ENCOUNTERS
—WITH—
WISDOM

ENCOUNTERS

—WITH—

WISDOM

❖ BOOK ONE ❖

Thomas Hora, M.D.

The PAGL Foundation
Old Lyme, CT

Published by the PAGL Foundation
P.O. Box 4001, Old Lyme, CT 06371

Copyright © 2006 by the PAGL Foundation.

Manufactured in the United States of America.

Library of Congress Cataloging-in-Publication Data

ISBN: 1-931052-03-4
LCCN: 2006901719

Contents

Introduction

This book is the first in a series of short volumes that continue to present Dr. Thomas Hora's Metapsychiatric teachings through dialogues with his students. Dr. Hora, the founder of Existential Metapsychiatry, was a pioneering psychiatrist who blended psychological knowledge with philosophical and spiritual wisdom. He passed away in 1995, and his work lives on.

This selection of dialogues from the 1980s and 1990s remains fresh and helpful. We are fortunate that Dr. Hora tape-recorded most of his weekly group sessions with his students and made them available to those who were there. The Board of the PAGL Foundation* has collected many of the tapes and transcribed some of them. They have then been carefully edited to guarantee participant anonymity, improve readability, coherence and relevance, and to assign a title to each based on the principal theme of each meeting.

At each session Dr. Hora would enter the room and sit at the front of a circle of students. He would quietly look around

---

*PAGL is an acronym for Peace, Assurance, Gratitude, and Love, qualities of consciousness that are the fruit of spiritual progress. The PAGL Foundation was established to make the work of Dr. Hora available. Previously published books consisting of group dialogues are *Dialogues in Metapsychiatry* and *One Mind*. Basic books by Dr. Hora on Existential Metapsychiatry are *Beyond the Dream* and *Existential Metapsychiatry*. These and other books and tapes are available from the PAGL Foundation and its bookstore (see *www.pagl.org*).

the room, smiling at each participant. Someone would begin by asking a question or presenting a problem. Sometimes no one spoke up and Dr. Hora began by seeking to discern what was on peoples' minds.

The dialogue proceeded with Dr. Hora encouraging the students to shed light on whatever issue had been raised, and shifted when some participant found the need to bring up another topic. Everything flowed, and there was never pressure to continue discussing any single issue. At the end of each session the students left with a new understanding.

Encounters in Wisdom is your invitation to join that dialogue.

I

Spiritual Blessedness

Student: I have a general, kind of vague comment that I cannot pin down to one particular question. A few weeks ago I spoke to my cousin. She is a widow, raising 4 boys, the eldest being about 30, and she was with him on Mother's Day. He has a boat and he took her out on the boat and to a restaurant and so on and so forth. Anyway, being a widow she has over the years been looking for a second husband and usually when we meet, what comes up in the conversation is, "Do you meet guys? Do you meet girls?" Anyway, this went on for a little bit, and then she said, "I feel as if life is passing me by." And she asked, "Do you feel the same way?" It troubled me and I think I said, "Yes." Now what does this mean, this phrase, because I find that often this comes up.

Dr. Hora: Yes. That is a very beautiful question, a philosophical question. You hear it very often and perhaps most people have the thought that life is passing them by. I'm getting older, and I am still not married and I still don't have a million dollars or a Jaguar, and I still don't have friends, or whatever life is supposed to have for me. This is called existential frustration. Life is passing me by. Well, on the face of it, if you cannot catch a man, if you don't get married, you miss out on life. If you don't have certain things you are failing. You are getting older and perhaps sickly and you have no sense of fulfillment. In earlier days they didn't speak about life passing you by, but how could I find fulfillment. Even in biblical times people were concerned about fulfillment. Fulfillment means living so that we do not have life passing us by. How could we really live life the way it should be lived? Right? And people do all kinds of things trying to prevent life from passing them by. They jump out of planes with parachutes. They try to have a lot of sex or money or power. Everybody clamors for a solution so that they wouldn't feel that they are missing out on life, and it is a great mystery. How can we live life in such a way as to not have this gnawing sense that life is passing us by? It is a very important philosophical question, something to ponder for everyone.

Most people will say there is no solution to this question. Anybody who would say that he is living life to the fullest is lying. Have you ever met somebody who would claim that he is living life to the full? Nobody. Apparently some people asked Jesus about this. You know that Jesus had an answer to every possible thing. There is no such question for which Jesus didn't have an answer. What was his answer? People asked him about this problem.

Student: "Blessed are they who hunger and thirst after righteousness for they will be filled" (Matt. 5:4).

Dr. Hora: Exactly. Did you know this? He always came up with a very simple answer to the most complicated question. "Blessed are they that hunger and thirst after righteousness: for they shall be fulfilled" (Matt 5:4). What does this mean? Let us look at this simple statement. In other words, if we would want to experience life in its fullness, a fully meaningful life, where we wouldn't have this fear of it passing us by, we wouldn't be afraid of dying prematurely or being sick or losing out on anything good that is rightfully ours, what is required? You have to hunger and thirst after righteousness. What the heck does that mean?

Student: Right seeing? Right usefulness?

Dr. Hora: Any other ideas, anybody?

Student: Well, right thinking.

Dr. Hora: Right thinking? Could you explain that?

Student: If our thoughts are valid, we are in a place of right being, right thinking.

Dr. Hora: Not quite.

Student: Righteousness is a very difficult word. It is a religious word.

Dr. Hora: You bet. That's why we are trying to understand it.

Student: Well, right thinking is holding in consciousness right values and right qualities and discerning spiritually that which is the good of God.

Dr. Hora: You see life is passing us by because we are not seeking what is existentially valid. We are preoccupied with trivial pursuits (laughter) . . . therefore we don't get it.

Student: Some people seem to get it.

Dr. Hora: Who is that?

Student: Well, I'll tell you. A few weeks ago I was on a hike with this woman. She was very verbal. You couldn't miss her.

Dr. Hora: Sounds like a liberated woman.

Student: She has a job as a VP with Chase Manhattan Bank. She is in charge of 50 people. She just got back from a month long trip to Europe where she combined it with business meetings and sightseeing. She has two houses, one in the country. She skis. She's a woman who speaks very clearly, has a sense of balance and she can talk on any number of subjects. And the way she handles herself made me say to myself, "Gees, this to me is a woman who seems to have made it."

Dr. Hora: So, if you could become such a woman (laughter), that would give meaning to your life and you wouldn't have this awful sense of life passing you by. Is this so?

Student: It wouldn't mean anything.

Other Student: But what I think you are saying is that these things do not seem like trivial pursuits.

Dr. Hora: Yes. Fifty people under you, two houses, skiing. You see, Jesus didn't know about these things. All he said was that you just have to desire the right things. You have to be interested in the right things. Otherwise we all have the sense of lack because we are pursuing existentially irrelevant values. See, if you have two houses, or three, or five, this isn't going to prolong your life or even give you PAGL (peace, assurance, gratitude and love); chances are it will give you more of a headache.

Student: Let me ask you this. If this woman who we could consider successful, if she were honest would she say that she too feels that life is passing her by?

Dr. Hora: Definitely. Or if she would deny it then she doesn't realize that life is passing her by. (laughter) What is life? What is it?

Student: We call it consciousness.

Dr. Hora: What is that?

Student: It is awareness and can be filled with either unreality or reality.

Dr. Hora: Yes. Well, simply, life is God. And God is life and if we are interested in life then we have to be interested in God. And if we are really interested in God, then life cannot pass us by because we are completely immersed in this life and the sayings of Jesus simply reiterate in different words the first principle of Metapsychiatry. Would you believe that? If you are primarily and wholeheartedly and unequivocally and absolutely interested in the first principle, which is the good of God, you will know life as spiritual blessedness and nothing in the world can give you a feeling of life passing you by. Because you are inseparably part of that life as long as you are aware of spiritual blessedness. This is life. As the Bible says, "This is life eternal, that they may know thee, the only true God, and Jesus Christ whom thou has sent" (John 17:3). So now life can be found in the first principle. You cannot sink your teeth into it, but that's life. Whatever is not spiritual blessedness is not life. It is the illusion of life. So when we hunger and thirst after righteousness we are interested in the good of God because that's the only reality. All the other things that we are interested in are not realities; they are just human values. Now what is wrong with human values? There's nothing wrong with being a VP and having two houses and skiing, and being well spoken. But human values can never give you a sense of fulfillment. How is that? Did you ever think of this? Human values can never give you a sense of fulfillment.

Student: Because you are really a spiritual being and you cannot look to another dimension or the human level. You cannot find your fulfillment as a spiritual being on the material level.

Dr. Hora: That's right exactly. And people are just clamoring for an endless variety of human experiences and that's not life; that is the dream of life in matter. The dream of life in the body, in clothes, in relationships, in interaction, in business, in a profession, all this is life in the material world. The material world is not real life.

Student: Dr. Hora, why are we not satisfied with what we have in the material world?

Dr. Hora: Why is one of the 6 dumb questions, right? And suppose you would be a new Jesus and say life is passing you by because you are not satisfied with your human values and all you need is to get somebody to make you satisfied, and then you have it made.

Student: Human values are always accompanied by interaction and that always involves comparison thinking. So how can we ever be satisfied when someone is always going to have more than we have of other things?

Dr. Hora: Well suppose you recognize that interaction is a human value and you can never find satisfaction with that. So you decide, as others have, to become a hermit and avoid contact with other people. Will that solve your problem? No. So a human being can never be free of this gnawing experience of life passing us by, because on the human plane we are all mortals and as long as we see ourselves as scheduled to die, how can anything make any sense? Human beings have a terminal disease. We are all scheduled to die. So life is not only a bore and a lousy drag, but it is also very short and dirty.

Student: And unfair.

Dr. Hora: So Jesus didn't say how a human being can find fulfillment. There is no such human experience that could lead to fulfillment. But spiritual blessedness is not a human experience. Did you ever think of that? And it is not unavailable. It's available.

Student: Evidently we have to hunger and thirst for it.

Dr. Hora: Yes, how do we do that?

Student: Recognize that we are not fulfilled.

Dr. Hora: Yes, so?

Student: We need to understand righteousness. We need to know what we need.

Dr. Hora: We need to know what is the right thing to long for, to be interested in.

Student: Hunger is longing. Is that correct?

Dr. Hora: Longing is a transitional thing. Longing can become very demanding or willful or aggressive. So we prefer the word interest. When we are hungry we are interested in food. When we are thirsty we are interested in beer. (laughter) But Jesus said, when we hunger and thirst after righteousness, we are interested in knowing the truth of life, which is synonymous with the good of God. The good of God is real life and the first principle can get us there, and to the extent that we learn spiritual blessedness we see the trivialness of everything else on the human scene, because nothing else can compare with that. So it is not an impossible thing to find fulfillment. But this fulfillment is spiritual.

Student: Dr. Hora, there is another passage in the bible that says not to take thought for all of these things but . . .

Dr. Hora: "Seek ye first the kingdom of God and his righteousness and all these things shall be added unto you" (Matt. 6:33). But you see we are not really going to waste time speculating about these other things, because we can very quickly be sidetracked. There are so many things on the human plane, and we can become mentally fixated on human values, like Marilyn Monroe or sex or money. If you then get hung up on these things, you completely lose sight of real value, of the real life. But on the real road to fulfillment you lose the sense that life is passing you by. There is no other way to be free of this thought that life is passing us by, except with an intimate acquaintance with the first principle and its blessing. Spiritual blessedness is the true sense of reality and it is absolutely good and it lifts us up to a higher level of appreciation of life that does not pass us by. The Bible also says, "When this mortal shall have put on immortality, then shall it come to pass, as it is written, death is swallowed up in victory" (1 Cor. 15:54).

Student: And this real life is spiritual.

Dr. Hora: That's exactly right, and with the help of the first principle, we can discover that as spiritual beings we are immortal; and when we catch a glimpse of this truth that real life can never die, that when the belief of mortality is replaced with the knowledge of immortality, then you see that life cannot pass us by. It ain't going anywhere. It's right there for ever. We are really immortal but we do not know it. We are convinced that we are mortals and the clock is ticking away toward the time when we will all die. But that dying is the dream of life on the human plane; that's material life.

Student: Can we talk about what it means to live in God's spiritual blessedness? What kind of thought is with you living in the spiritual world?

Dr. Hora: That's a good question. Can anybody understand this?

Student: That we are blessed spiritually, which means we are blessed with the ideas needed to live life harmoniously.

Dr. Hora: Yes, that we are at one with that life which is God. "I and my Father are one" (John 10:30). "I am in the Father and the Father is in me" (John 14:10). In spiritual blessedness this is clear. We are aware of it. This is so. There are not two things — God and man. There is only God as man, and man as an individualized aspect of God. But most people do not stop to think about it. They say, "Let's have fun." Who will bother with these philosophical speculations? And then what did Jesus know anyway? He didn't even have a credit card. (laughter)

Student: I thought he was the first guy with unlimited credit. (more laughter)

Student: Dr. Hora, it is a little unclear to me what actually gets us there. There is a requirement that there be a sincere interest in God, and at our level, that seems to take the form of monitoring our thoughts and becoming aware of invalid thoughts and then either discarding them or allowing valid thoughts to enter consciousness. Is that the same thing as being sincerely interested or is that something that we are required to do because we seem to be human and then we become interested? What comes first? The interest or this process that we are required to go through?

Dr. Hora: This is not a process we are talking about now. We are talking about an opening that is available to everybody, an opening into enlightenment and immortality. You know Sartre's play, "No Exit." He didn't think that there was an exit from the human condition, and most people don't. But we must not let that stop us. There is an exit at hand, available to everybody ever since Jesus Christ walked on the earth, and Metapsychiatry was inspired with the Eleven Principles. So we are not hopeless cases stuck in the human condition. There is an exit door and it is called the First Principle of Metapsychiatry. So it is not a process; it's just facing up to the meaning of this principle. When we do we discover that all of these tremendous philosophical problems that philosophers for thousands of years have been agonizing over have resolved themselves into a very simple crack in reality. And

Jesus Christ gave the world a very simple statement. "Blessed are they who hunger and thirst after righteousness, for they shall find fulfillment." And we say that if we are truly, and above all else, interested in the good of God, we discover spiritual blessedness and we can see that this is qualitatively entirely different from everything the world considers good and of value. There is no material element in it. It is pure spiritual realization. And if we get acquainted with this truth, the good of God, we don't have to live in fear of dying. We will know that the phenomena of death are just phenomena. In phenomenology there are two factors: appearance and disappearance. The phenomenal life, which we consider is passing us by, is just appearance and disappearance. Now what happens when an appearance disappears?

Student: Our seeing improves.

Dr. Hora: You know what happens? Nothing. (laughter)

Student: Because it never was.

Dr. Hora: Right. So if there is a phenomenon, then it is part of the phenomenon where we are appearing to be and then we are not appearing to be. Nothing has changed. Life is unaffected. God hasn't changed. Reality is still there and we are in it. So life cannot pass us by. We can have the impression that life is passing us by, but nobody can actually miss out on life. When we wake up to the first principle it is like an awakening. "This is life eternal that they may know thee the only true God, and Jesus Christ, whom thou hast sent" (John 17:3).

Student: So what is the meaning of appearing and disappearing?

Dr. Hora: That's a phenomenon. A phenomenon is an observable something where we can see thoughts taking on shape and losing shape.

Student: But, a tree is not a thought, is it?

Dr. Hora: Sure it is. What else is a tree it but a thought?

Student: Whose thought?

Dr. Hora: Everybody who looks at it. The material world is called the phenomenal world. Everything is made of thoughts; trees are made of thoughts, animals are made of thoughts, people are made of thoughts, and they are forever appearing and disappearing. That's what mortality is, the disappearance of appearances.

Student: So that's mortality?

Dr. Hora: Well, it's a human illusion, an impression, here today and gone tomorrow. (laughter)

Student: Where is the spirituality in the phenomena?

Dr. Hora: There is no spirituality in the phenomena.

Student: Then where is it? What is it? If we appear and disappear with thoughts manifesting and not manifesting, so where is the spiritual then?

Dr. Hora: Right there! Spiritual reality is all encompassing. Divine Mind fills the whole universe, right there where the phenomena are.

Student: Even with the phenomena?

Dr. Hora: Phenomena don't take up space. They just seem to take up space. In divine reality there is plenty of parking space. There is no crowding whatsoever. (laughter) Time and space do not exist. These are mind-boggling ideas, but you can get used to them. Just don't tell anybody. (laughter)

Student: It's interesting that in physics, first the direction was that everything was solid and then they taught us that there are atoms in constant motion.

Dr. Hora: Yes, it's vibrations. It's waves. It's particles turning into waves and waves turning into particles. It is nothing solid. The only solid thing is love. Divine love fills the whole universe. It is infinite omnipresence. It is so solid you could cut it with a knife if you had a spiritual knife.

Something needs to be clarified. What is the practical value of contemplating what we were talking about now? Suppose our friend here should go on a hike next week and this woman should tell you all of her accomplishments. Would you be impressed the same way as you were?

Student: Well I might be, but I would have foreknowledge.

Dr. Hora: Yes. You see, if we have some idea of the first principle and divine reality, then we cannot become so frustrated about all the things that other people seem to have and we don't have. Right? Nowadays envy has become so blatant. The culture is so filled with envy and jealousy and rivalry that people are tremendously eager to find fulfillment in life. So men undergo sex change operations because they want to have what women have. Have you noticed how many men wear ponytails and earrings, lately, and all kinds of things? Culturally, people envy each other, and they try to be what somebody else is, and it is a very disquieting life that most people live, because wherever you look you see somebody that has something that you don't have, and you are forever looking for it. For example, if I would only have bigger breasts then I would be fulfilled with a fullness of the bosom. (laughter) So many women rush to the surgeons and have implants put into their breasts with sometimes disastrous consequences. This is what you brought up today. Life is very disquieting and we are troubled because we are unfulfilled and have the sense that we are missing out on something and this leads to rivalries and all kinds of problems. Nobody is at peace, and nobody is satisfied. Nobody is happy; nobody is really joyous. Even when you go on a hike you have to listen to a woman tell you all the things that she has.

Student: Bragging.

Dr. Hora: Bragging, showing off, self-confirmation, interaction, rivalry: that's the human condition, various kinds of distortions, existentially invalid interests that lead to trouble. But if you really understand what fulfillment is, and how you can get there, you will be more peaceful and you will not suffer so much from all the things you do not have. And you won't get such a kick out of what you have, but you won't suffer for not having.

Student: I would be interested in hearing more about right seeing. You said, "The way you see the tree." And someone, a Buddhist monk, posited this the other night, that President Bush [the elder] is the embodiment of the consciousness of America, and that until the consciousness of the people changes, where there is more right seeing of that which peace really is, there will not be peace. Now, the tree, when you look at the tree, everything is embodied in the tree, and you had a koan once that the tree is in the leaf, and I would like you to help me see spiritually.

Dr. Hora: Well you brought up certain things, like the Buddhist Monk. Where shall we start? Shall we start with the President? Is Bush the embodiment of the consciousness of America? No. Only the Republican Party. (laughter) And what is the consciousness of America? More and more goodies, here and there some political freedom and also Christian values permeating the culture. But you cannot make a sweeping statement that Bush is the consciousness of America. That is a simplification. He is the President of the United States. He is a Republican and his thoughts and values are imbued by everything America stands for and what the Republican Party stands for, etc. Now when we look at a tree, what do we see?

Student: What we think we see in the tree.

Dr. Hora: That's right. We see our own thoughts about the trees, and they can be as varied as people vary. There is a spiritual interpretation of nature, which includes trees, and also people and animals, that everything on the planet earth is a symbolic structure pointing towards God-except a rotten tree. Anything healthy, anything beautiful, anything that uplifts the spirit is a symbolic structure pointing toward God. Now you asked about seeing or the question of eyesight?

Student: Well, there are thoughts about eyesight with me, but also about right seeing. That was where we started in the beginning, and I need to learn about right seeing.

Dr. Hora: We have the prayer of right seeing: "Everything and everyone is here for God whether they know it or not." What is everything? Trees, art, monuments, houses, dogs and cats, life forms, all kinds of values. Everything is here for God in a symbolic way. Now what Metapsychiatry teaches is a direct awareness of God and of ourselves in the context of God. This is where fulfillment can be found, when we find that we are all individual aspects of infinite mind, which is God; and to the extent that we can understand this, we have transcended the world. Because God is life and life never dies and anyone who knows himself as being an inseparable aspect of infinite mind also knows that he can never die. And that reminds us of what Jesus said, "I am the resurrection and the life; he that believeth in me, though he were dead, yet shall he live, and whosoever liveth and believeth in me shall never die" (John 11:25). So that's it. As far as having good eyesight, it is very important to see clearly what life is and what life isn't and that helps the eyesight. In studying Metapsychiatry, some students discover that their eyesight improves to such a point that they are able to discard their glasses. Many miraculous things happen here; yet nobody brags about it. But every time we become a little more grateful or humble, a little more spiritually minded, something good happens. It is amazing.

2

The Inside and the Outside

Student: Dr. Hora, this past year there has been a lot of destruction when it comes to weather. Now the floods in Mississippi and you know the whole Midwest and earlier storms during the winter and in thinking about it, you watch one disastrous news thing after another and you can't help but wonder. I mean it seems like we go from one disaster to another and it's affecting so many. And it's devastating for those that are . . .

Dr. Hora: How could we improve this situation?

Student: It has got to be that some kind of mental climate has to change.

Dr. Hora: Right. What did Jesus say about the weather bureau? (laughter) He said the Kingdom of God will come when the inside will be outside and the outside will be inside. (From, I think, the Gospel According to Thomas, The Gnostic Sayings of Jesus) That's when the Kingdom of God will be here. And everything will be permanently harmonious. Do you believe that? What did he mean by saying, "When the inside will be outside and the outside will be inside?"

Student: Does it mean, when a man realizes that what he experiences is a consequence of his thoughts.

Dr. Hora: Right. It is not just a consequence; it is the thoughts. For it says when we experience storms it means that we are involved with thoughts, stormy thoughts, conflict, fears, aggression, hatred, jealousy, right? And everything we experience is according to our thoughts, individually and collectively.

Student: I am not clear about that. In a city racked with tornados, or a major storm like a hurricane, I assume that not everybody in the city is in a mental state of turmoil. Yet everybody in the city is affected by the storm. How does that work? Are innocent people affected as well?

Dr. Hora: Sure. Do you remember the story of Noah? What does the story of Noah tell us about the weather, or floods? What does it say? Do you know the story of Noah? (Gen. 6–9).

Student: I guess a little bit.

Dr. Hora: Tell us what you do know.

Student: I just know that he was told to build a boat.

Dr. Hora: You already have the boat and in the Mississippi there are floods. So you didn't fix it. Do you think these are irrelevant stories in the Bible, or do they have some actual relevancy to daily experience?

Student: I thought that you were going to tell us the story about the ten righteous men. I don't recall the specifics of the story. Something about the city was saved or would be saved if you could find one righteous man (Eccles. 9:15).

Dr. Hora: Yes. Did they find him?

Student: I think so.

Dr. Hora: In Noah's time there was a lot of pornography and prostitution and killings and murders and sexual excesses. The whole community was demoralized and they turned away from the truth of God. And the result was that the whole area was completely flooded and everybody died. Only Noah's family survived and some of the animals that he took into the boat survived. Now this tells us something. The mental climate was corrupt and people were self righteous and aggressive and cursing and crime prevailed and disaster followed. Because what is outside is inside and what is inside is outside. Now we cannot do very much with what is outside but we can improve what is inside. How is that? You see when 2 and 2 is 4 then 2 million and 2 million will be . . . can you calculate?

Student: Without a computer?

Dr. Hora: Four million. So it is very important to work on behalf of God, which means to help the world individually and in small groups or larger groups to realize the importance of right understanding of God. We are not just helplessly sitting by. It is possible to improve the situation by focusing our attention on infinite mind. As Einstein told us, the divine mind is the harmonizing principle of the universe. We start out with our individual problems, and as we grow in understanding we become beneficial presences in the world in proportion to how well we have learned to assume responsibility for our thoughts.

People usually ask, "What can we do?" What should we do? What is to be done? There are tremendous problems in the world. In Tokyo they are having problems and in The Bronx. But Jesus put it very simply. He had a way of putting it right on the line. What is inside is outside and what is outside is inside.

Student: So, when we see these reports...but I don't see how...if the news constantly creates more fear by "oh they expect another swelling of water and more rain," people can't help but be in a panic. We can see it in our consciousness and we can come to realize that it is a manifestation of invalid thoughts.

Dr. Hora: Yes.

Student: And that is all that we can do.

Dr. Hora: Yes. I know a man who had to go to a doctor for an insurance physical exam. During the examination the doctor took his blood pressure and said it is alarming how high your blood pressure is. Your blood pressure is alarmingly high. So what happened? He got alarmed. He got so alarmed that his blood pressure continued to shoot up. And then the doctor said, "Well, this is what we are going to do about it. I'll give you a blood pressure machine and twice a day you are going to measure your blood pressure and write it down on a piece of paper and then you will bring it to me after a few weeks."

Student: Torture.

Dr. Hora: And we will see how the blood pressure is affecting you and what we can do. And certainly every time he measured his blood pressure it was worse and worse and worse and he was living with fear all this time. I don't know what happened later on. He was probably given some drugs. And the drugs say this — all drugs are listening to St. Paul's principle. What is St. Paul's principle? "The good which I would I do not; but the evil which I would not, that I do" (Rom. 7:19). This is St. Paul's principle. And that's how things work on an individual basis and on a collective basis and with the great blessings of technological progress with which we can communicate with millions of people instantaneously. We don't have to go from community to community in Mississippi and scare people by saying, "Listen, there will be a flood," because it's time already to have a flood. So everybody gets the bad news right away. We have the great privilege through the blessings of technological progress to get alarmed collectively at the same time. That's the way it works. Alarmed. We have to be alarmed. I understand that goes with everything. The stock market goes up and people get enthusiastic. The next day it goes down and people get alarmed. They run here and they run there investing and disinvesting. I like to listen to these financial advisors; no matter what the situation, they always end up saying but it's a good time to buy stocks. Right? Invariably they wind up recommending stocks to buy. This is a good opportunity to buy and people buy and then they sell. That's the way it is. And everyone lives in fear that doesn't understand the teachings of Jesus. Whether you're a financier or whatever you are, if you do not understand, then you live in fear. And the Bible says, "Fear not little flock, for it is your Father's good pleasure to give you the kingdom" (Luke 12:32). Would you believe this? Would anyone believe it that God is giving us the kingdom? What is this kingdom? In the kingdom of God, nobody has to be afraid. There is peace, assurance, gratitude and love. "For the earth shall be full of the knowledge of the Lord, as the waters cover the sea" (Isa. 11:9).

Student: What does that mean?

Dr. Hora: Well, when the truth of God's reality will be known throughout the world then there will be peace and freedom. There will be no fear and no gnashing of teeth. Somewhere in the Bible there is this phrase "gnashing of the teeth" (Matt. 8:12). But don't tell it to a dentist because he will say you need implants right away, or root canal.

There are some of these pharmaceutical advertisements that are fantastic. There are two young, beautiful, healthy, teenage girls and one says, "I have a headache." The other says right away, "Take two, take two." What two? Two Anacin tablets, two, right away. She was all prepared with medical advice. She knows what to do if you have a headache. Nobody asks the question what is this headache all about. No, the remedy is quickly to take two. There are many such advertisements, which are very, very funny. Except when they are disgusting because they intimidate people.

There is a funny thing going on now. We have heard a great deal about the shortage of doctors. There is a shortage of doctors. People are standing in line to get an appointment and they live in fear they will not be able to get medical help. And you open the papers and especially the professional papers and it is full of advertisements about doctors in groups, which have wonderful new equipment and they can help you right away. Now there is a surplus of available medical help because they expect that changes will take place throughout the health care systems and they want to get in on the bonanza. The bonanza consists of the people who will be rushing to sign up with doctors and get insurance in case there will be a shortage. The public is being intimidated about the shortage of doctors and the doctors are constantly being encouraged to advertise. How do these doctors advertise? They advertise, "We have a new machine for hemorrhoids. Immediate help is available." Also there is laser surgery and all kinds of things. As a medical man, I have never heard of these diseases they come up with that they are advertising as instantly available. You can have miracle cures with all kinds of technological things. Today I saw an advertisement that says, "I am a noninvasive surgical specialist. I specialize in noninvasive surgery. You don't have to be afraid. You just come to me and I will fix it." What's going on? They know that people are afraid of the invasive manner in which they are making tests and here is a guy who is asking for more patients, more business and advertising himself as a noninvasive surgeon. And the *New York Times* has an article that for a long time people went to a doctor and the doctor wanted to help the patient out of the goodness of his heart. And then there came a time when the doctors wanted to show their diagnostic abilities, that they could find the most fantastic diseases that nobody ever thought of. So first it was the patient who was the focus. Then the sickness was the issue. But now we have made so much progress that neither the patient nor the sickness matters. What matters now is procedure. Doctors are interested in procedures. What does that mean? They want to do something to you because that's where the insurance money comes from. Diagnosis doesn't matter. The human being doesn't matter. The opportunity for procedures is what is important. So you go to a doctor and he wants to figure out how could I find a way to justify my eagerness to make a procedure because that's where the money is. It's a terrible, terrible situation and I don't know how this is going to end up. But people are very upset, very fearful and justifiably so. You have the ethical standing of doctors now on the level of used car salesmen.

One of our friends here went on a vacation and said, "Before I go on my vacation I am going to have a check up." Smart people recommend this. An intelligent person, before he goes on vacation goes to the doctor for a check up just in case something is wrong, right? Reasonable. So she went to a doctor who found nothing. But he said, "Now let's try a blood test." He takes her blood, looks under a microscope and says, "There is something strange about the platelets in the blood." Do you know what platelets are? They are really insignificant. They are for clotting; they're responsible for clotting. And he said, "Well, when you come back from the vacation we will have to look into these platelets." The patient started to be worried about these platelets and I was hearing about these platelets for weeks on end and her endless worrying. So she got another test, another examination about the platelets in her blood. And so, again, they found nothing wrong with her platelets. And then something went wrong with her pocketbook. $300 for a visit to the platelets specialist who discovered that there was nothing wrong with the patient. By this time she was probably glad to pay the $300 and make an end to the platelets business. That's the way things are done today. So next time you go for a check up leave your platelets at home. (laughter) Every time I hear people tell me they went for a check up they come back with something. There is a man who went for a check up and they couldn't find anything and

they kept reassuring him, "Don't worry, we'll find something."
(laughter)

Student: How do we know when we've reached the point
where we don't have to go for a checkup?

Dr. Hora: Is there anything in the American constitution, by
the founding fathers of the United States of America that
we have to go for a check up? If in Czechoslovakia people
go for checkups, I would be surprised. But you cannot say to
somebody go or don't go. Nobody can say that. We have to
assume responsibility for having an open mind and trying to
understand our situation in life and making our decisions on
the information we gather somehow. So when we speak about
this, we don't say don't go to the doctor; neither do we say go
to the doctor. We say, ask your advisor. Who is our advisor?
Divine love is our advisor. Divine love always tells us what we
need to know provided we have learned to hear its voice. If
we have not learned to hear its voice, we have to listen to all
kinds of other advice and that can be frightening sometimes.
"He that hath an ear, let him hear..." (Rev.2:7). This is such
a mystical saying, isn't it? How are the platelets?

Maybe I didn't tell you the whole quotation. "The kingdom
of God will come when the inside will be outside and the
outside will be inside and the two shall be one" (The Gnostic
Gospel According to Thomas, Log 22).

Student: So we come to realize that we are divine consciousness.

Dr. Hora: Exactly.

Student: So we are not invalid or valid, but divine.

Dr. Hora: Yes. What does it mean that the two shall be one?

Student: Rather than being separate, rather than our experiences in our life being separate from our thoughts; our thoughts determine our experiences; they are our experiences. They are not independent entities that occur without each other.

Dr. Hora: Well, if we look at ourselves and at others from a human standpoint, according to appearances, we see that everyone is a bag made of skin. And in this bag there are all kinds of junk and this bag contains all kinds of thoughts and these thoughts can be expressed outwardly. See? We have the impression that we are thinking inside and we are expressing these self-generated thoughts from the inside to the outside and this is our life. If you are successful in expressing your insides on the outside and you manage your life somehow to work, then you say, "Well, my thoughts have helped me to manage my life in a certain way due to my expressing to the outside what is inside." Now of course Jesus says that's not really so. It just seems that way. Actually all is one. The Bible says, "Hear oh Israel: The Lord our God is one God" (Deut. 6:4). What does that mean? It means that all there is anywhere in the universe is the divine mind, infinite mind, consciousness. There is no inside, no outside. There is wisdom, there is love, there is beauty, there is goodness, there is freedom, there is joy and there are cats and dogs. But all is one. Consciousness is all there is. And our lives seem to be oriented towards becoming acquainted with the reality of consciousness. So all will be one. We just have to learn to be aware of God as the harmonizing principle of the universe.

Student: This reminds me of the comment from Zen: form is formlessness and formlessness is form. Isn't that the same idea?

Dr. Hora: Yes.

Student: Because at that point, it's non-dimensional. What you're saying is that all is one.

Dr. Hora: Jesus said that. Imagine if everybody could understand this. Here comes the teacher upon the world scene and he gives us this information. The inside is outside, the outside is inside, and all is one. And then he says, "I am come that they may have life and that they might have it more abundantly" (John 10:10). So if we listen to his teachings and gain some understanding there will be abundance of good in the world. And many of these sayings are oriented to help the human race to find goodness in life and health and freedom and wisdom. But this teacher was a unique teacher. He didn't waste one word ever in his teaching. Whenever he said something, it was an utterance. No ifs and buts. He just uttered the truth appropriate to the occasion. That's a unique teacher, an existential teacher who doesn't talk too much. At one point he said, "Love not the world, neither the things that are in the world for he that loveth the world, the love of the Father is not in him" (1 John 2:15).

That reminds me, I was watching television a few days ago and on one of these talk shows they had two rabbis. Hassidic rabbis. They were sitting in black hats and there were parents there, and they all were having troubles with their children. They asked these rabbis what about your children and they said, "Our children have no problems; they have no contact with the world. We have no television. They don't listen to the radio. They just live in the context of our religion and laws of our religion. And the children are happy and very healthy and the families have no problems." They are so-called "observant Jews." The parents asked them if they missed the television, the radio, rock and roll. Don't they want these things? Oddly enough, those children are not interested in these things and they are never sick; they have no family crises. And, standing out in the group of families who were all having all kinds of problems with their children were these two guys in their black hats, who come up and say we haven't had any problems with our children.

So, what is one to think about this? They have an ethical code which is five thousand years old and has not been perverted or contaminated by technological problems. Of course these are the rabbis and they have a value system that has worked through the ages. To us they seem to be sort of obscure and outdated but nevertheless in the context of their community it works by the sheer avoidance of the world. So Jesus said, "Love not the world or the things that are in the world. For he that loveth the world, the love of the Father is not in him" (1 John 2:15). It was a very strange saying. Jesus said, "Don't love the world." Here the great lover says don't love the world. It really means don't swallow any kind of value the world is throwing at you. But the world says you have to keep up with the Joneses and you have to be hip; if you are not in you are out, yes? You have to conform to the world; otherwise you are a failure. And then the Bible says, "Be not conformed to this world, but be ye transformed by the renewing of your mind, that ye may prove what is that good, and acceptable, and perfect, will of God" (Rom. 12:2).

Student: Dr. Hora, in that other passage it says we are in the world but not of it. Is it even possible for us to leave the world?

Dr. Hora: We don't leave the world; we just refuse to buy it.

Student: Because we are in it.

Dr. Hora: No, if you go to Bloomingdale's, do you have to buy everything they are selling? No. Do you have to go gaga over the lingerie or whatever? We are in the world but not of it. And even if something is very popular you don't have to buy it. You can see it and you can be aware of the fact that many of the values that are being offered to us in very clever ways are existentially invalid. We don't have to buy it. Now suppose there is a famous psychotherapist in California and he has come up with an ingenious way of helping his patients by arranging for them to have their group sessions in a swimming pool naked. It sounds very exciting, no? You don't have to buy it, right? They are actually doing this in California.

The famous guru Ragneesh started his work in this country in Oregon. He had special groups where people were raping, beating, and fighting with each other. And he recommended that people go through the experience of being abused psychologically and physically and sexually. And they even photographed it. And Ragneesh said this is good. You have to go through this experience. But there were many people who got very excited, thinking that this would be an interesting experience. Even one of our friends was initially very tempted to go there and be exposed to these carnal kinds of orgies that he had there. I think later on they stopped it because it was such a dangerous temptation. But you see that when you are in the world and you love the world, you long for what's in this world and you can really go very far on the road to self-destruction. So don't be surprised when Jesus said, "Love not the world or the things that are in the world."

Student: Is that what it means that you can't serve two masters? Is that the idea, that if we love the world then that is a kind of master to us. Then we are not loving God, which is the real master? There is a biblical passage that says we can't serve two masters because if we serve one then we hate the other. I was trying to understand it.

Dr. Hora: Well, it is very clear that you can't worship two gods. But this is more than that. You can say, well, I don't worship two gods, I only worship one and that is pornography or something like that. Now, do you think God is squeamish and He doesn't like it if you are engaged in certain value systems? It's not that God is not interested; it means that God's value system, the spiritual system of existentially valid values cannot help you because you are interested in what is not valid. So the good of God is not available to you because you are ignoring it. It's always available if you sincerely turn to those values and rearrange your life to conform to what is healthy and intelligent. But this is not a matter of competition between God and man. It's just that if we are distracted we don't benefit from the presence of God because we are turning our backs on God.

Student: Dr. Hora, is there any kind of healthy interaction if interaction is two people sitting and talking to each other?

Dr. Hora: There is neither healthy nor unhealthy interaction. It just ain't. It's an emotion. It doesn't exist. There is only omni-action, which means God is the only activating power of all that is real and good in the whole universe. It's the grid. Do you remember the grid? Einstein came up with this idea that the grid indicates the curvature of the universe. Which is just another way of saying God governs. The whole universe is under divine control and power. Of course normally we don't see it. He was able to make a statement about it because he had figured it out mathematically with paper and pencil. That this grid is responsible for what we see as gravitation. Now I was always, from childhood on secretly hoping that someone would figure out a way of eliminating gravity and we could float and fly and get around like Jesus did. You know, he could transport himself instantaneously from one place to another. Well, this far Einstein has not yet come. We have to be satisfied with a phone line.

Student: Did Jesus actually transport himself?

Dr. Hora: I was watching him do it. (laughter) Well, look here. Today we have television and instantaneously we can see what is happening in Tokyo. Isn't that fantastic? Not that this is spiritual, but the idea of the possibility of overcoming time and space is indicative of the direction in which humanity is moving.

Student: But is the idea that enabled television to do what it does, a spiritual idea?

Dr. Hora: The ideas come from the divine Mind and the human tendency is to destroy it and to pervert it. Every good idea that comes to us from the divine Mind sooner or later gets perverted to serve the devil.

Student: So how do you keep it pure so that it doesn't get perverted?

Dr. Hora: Well, we have a teacher sent from God. His name was Jesus Christ. He told us what is pure, what is good and what is true. In Metapsychiatry, we speak of what is existentially valid.

Student: When two people are having an argument we say it looks as if it's interaction. And you say there is no interaction. What is going on here?

Dr. Hora: Nothing, absolutely nothing. There are two people participating in an illusion of personal mind power. And there is no such thing. All action is derived from the divine Mind. And all wisdom and truth and love and energy come from the divine mind. So when we say there is only omni-action every-where we make a statement about the nature of divine reality. Infinite mind, which Einstein called the grid, governs every-thing that really is. Human perceptions are inaccurate, twisted, and pervert everything that is from God and good because we don't perceive the truth with our sensory equipment and with our intellect. We are unable to perceive God and God's uni-verse. It is only through cultivating another faculty that God is available to us if we are interested. Anybody who is interested can cultivate this faculty of spiritual awareness. And this is the avenue through which we can know the truth of God and the wisdom and the love that God is. So we always focus attention on what is, rather than on what should be or what shouldn't be, or what (what is the name of that Sufi comedian?) Nasrudin said. Do you all know of Nasrudin? He is a very interesting fellow. But we will have to talk about him another time.

3

Death and Mourning

Student: Dr. Hora, before I came to see you on Sunday I was going to use a different car to drive to your house and the battery was dead. So I used the other car and I came and saw you, and then I went home and later on that day I went outside and there was a dead mouse.

Dr. Hora: A dead mouse. Not a dead bird but a dead mouse.

Student: Then I started thinking to myself, "Well, the battery is dead, and the mouse is dead, and I really don't know what the meaning of it is." I do know that I spoke to my mother (laughter) on Sunday before I saw the dead mouse. I am just saying it this way because I think it might help to understand the meaning. The moment I heard her voice I knew that she was desperate for consolation. I guess that would be the right word. You know she is still very upset about her car accident and she is afraid to drive, and I guess she wants me to worry about her. That's what she wants, but I didn't think that I was worrying. I was aware that she was very needy, and I listened and I tried to pray. So I don't know if that is related to the needing. I really don't know what the meaning is.

Dr. Hora: Does anybody know? Do you know?

Student: The only thing that comes to mind is what you told me before when I described an incident where I saw a dead bird but it was someone else's meaning. You said it was based on interaction thinking. So I guess it has to be the same. It is some kind of interactive thought that must be taking place between her and her mother. I am not sure what that thought is but the battery went dead before she spoke to her mother. (laughter) Mother is always with us, right?

Student: Is it the idea that if she lets go of her mother there is a sense of death for one of them? Somehow it has to be connected with the idea that one of them has to die.

Dr. Hora: What do you think (addressing the original questioner)?

Student: These people use the expression: "You are killing me." It's an expression.

Student: It does seem that as long as the attachment between my mother and I exists, I have no freedom, and in that sense, I feel dead.

Dr. Hora: You feel dead?

Student: Many times I have said to you, "There is somebody here." It is as if I don't know who I am, and there is somebody who wants to break free, but it just doesn't seem possible.

Dr. Hora: To break free is not possible?

Student: Right. And to that extent, I am dead.

Dr. Hora: Yes.

Student: When one individual is under the domination of another's thoughts, there is no freedom at all. There can't be. It's impossible. When we are attached to something, I guess we can cherish it, hate it and fear it at the same time. There has to be a turning of attention over to God so that we can get closer to God and sort of get further away from our attachment. I guess there is no other solution than that.

Student: When I first came to you, Dr. Hora, many years ago, I could not leave my family, my mother and father. I was sure they would die if I left. There was no doubt in my mind that's what would happen and I could not leave them, and then I did and my mother and father got along much better. (laughter) It was such a shock to point out that they were really happier when I left, and there was less arguing between them, but it took me a long, long time to leave. I think that death thing is always there. If you think you are keeping someone alive by being attached to them, then you are sure they are going to die if you detach yourself.

Dr. Hora: So then the problem is this: When we see this phenomenon, we know that phenomena are thoughts, and they come to us when we find coexistence as robbing us of our lives, our freedom. Life is freedom and interestingly, many people have these experiences where they see somebody die, or somebody is about to die, or somebody is escaping from some accident. So the precariousness of life always comes into focus in one way or another, and Freud believed that there is a force of death called Thanatos. It's a Greek word for the God of death. A preoccupation with death can have a disguised form in terms of all kinds of thoughts, like dead car batteries or dead birds. People are involved in symptoms of hatred. Inexplicable thoughts of hatefulness all leave signs, but the best way to think of it is that we have a thought that we are not really free and we don't know that freedom is possible as long as certain people are in our proximity or we are involved in interacting with people. As an example, one of our members in the group went through a period of about four weeks of severe pain in the body. All these things are discordant thoughts revolving around the issue of freedom. So people who love each other and want to be close to each other also feel that situation as an enslavement of some kind and we are robbed of our freedom.

Freud spoke about the death wish: the wish to be dead for oneself or for somebody else. So when you love somebody, you also hate them, and you may be preoccupied mentally with such aggressively hostile thoughts, and then you don't want to know about it because it is not nice, right? It is important not to be afraid of it and confront it because it is altogether human. For unenlightened people it is impossible to love somebody without hating them and the more passionately we love somebody, the more we are inclined to hate them, and we are not aware of it emotionally. We can become aware of it in terms of symbolic images which occur mostly when we are asleep. In our sleep we can hate people, because we can say I don't have this dream. This is not my dream. I don't hate anybody. I love my mother, my sister, my father. I love everybody, just like the Bible says we have to, right? So the recommendation here is, don't be afraid of the truth. Don't deny it. Don't brag about it. Face it. It is a human condition. It is really nothing. In the final analysis, it is nothing because only God is reality and these symptoms are just dreams. Suppose you are dreaming that your loved one is dying, or is dead or is going to die? What if you would like him to die? It is really nothing. It is just something that you have come to believe, and that it is not nice. It is not nice to have such thoughts and people are afraid of them and they don't dare to face them. Consequently, you remain enslaved to the idea that you are a vitally important person who must maintain the status quo. If you hate somebody in the family, you have to convince yourself it is not true and that you really love them. So people struggle with all kinds of symptoms. Every night there is another ache and pain here and there. You are just struggling against Thanatos, the death wish towards someone you are supposed to love.

This is particularly clear when a loved one has died and you are left mourning and grieving and the grief has to be deep and public and noticeable because the measure of your love is in terms of the intensity of your grief. When somebody is grieving, people say how he loved her or how she loved him, how much love there was in this marriage. But the fact is that besides God, there is nothing, and we have to face the fact that on the human level we cannot love, because we want too much for ourselves. How can we love somebody if we want something from them? So, don't be afraid to face the truth that the human being is completely corrupt, and that is how you can set yourself on the path of liberation. We hear so much between husband and wife, friends and enemies. People develop these negative involvements where they claim that they are loving and actually find in their dreams that they are wishing them to drop dead. So nobody loves anybody. God is Love and that is sufficient. St. Paul complained to God that he had a thorn in his side and it wasn't going away, that it wasn't getting healed. He said, "What should I do?" and God said: Nothing, "my grace is sufficient for thee" (2 Cor. 12:9). So we are left with the reality of God's infinite, loving presence and everything then disappears. We can sleep better at night. It took me two years to sleep through a night. It is inevitable. Everybody gets it sooner or later. But if you know that this is nothing to be ashamed of, neither to be proud of, nor be afraid of, then you look at it face to face and see that this is not reality. This is self-preoccupation. It doesn't have to be. We have to let go of it to recapture our freedom.

Student: On the human level, if we love someone, we enslave them.

Dr. Hora: Sure.

Student: I spoke to a mother last year who told me at a parent conference how much she loved her children. She went on and on about how she devoted herself to them. They are her whole life. She loves them and then she says "but every summer I send them to California because I need some freedom." (laughter) That sounded so ridiculous, but now it really makes sense.

Dr. Hora: You get hooked on this idea that we can love humanly in an unadulterated fashion, and we are responsible for being loving all the time even toward our enemies. "Love thine enemies," says the Bible. Bless them that curse you, do good to them that hate you, and blame yourself for whatever happens. (laughter)

Student: What does that mean to love your enemies? I guess it means what you said before that the only love there is is that God is Love.

Dr. Hora: In the final analysis, God says that 2,000 years from now you will find out that there is no interaction anywhere; there is only omni-action everywhere. If you understand this principle, it will shorten the period of mourning.

Student: Everything you said sounds very much like compassion. You are saying you don't judge and you don't blame. But how is one to work with this idea? I know it's only a thought, this phenomenon, this emotion. It seems that that is what ties people in. The emotion seems to be the logical compassion, yet then you might be feeling that it's not me. But I am feeling her pain, her suffering, her loneliness and I know I go through this too. In other words, how do you cut that off because you feel like you're responsible and it's very tricky?

Dr. Hora: Just because you feel something is no proof of its reality. So don't kid yourself. Many people think that because I feel this and I feel that then that's for real. Fortunately we understand that feelings and emotions are just thoughts. Thoughts can come to us on the level of feelings, emotions and insights. It is all in the domain of feelings because nothing is really real except the truth. Truth is not an emotion. It is a thought and we have to learn not to be afraid of thoughts and not to exaggerate their importance. There is just the deceptive human consciousness. So we must not overestimate the importance of thoughts or feelings and emotions. Thoughts are the all important factor in life, and if we understand thoughts, we do not become enslaved by emotions. I feel. We always talk about how somebody makes us feel, or how an event made me feel so bad. I felt so bad. We like to talk about our feelings, and it is just self-confirmatory ideation, as you know. You cannot be free as long as you are enslaved by your emotions or feelings or memories. We take notice that we had this dream, this horrible dream about two birds dying on the rooftop. You didn't create these birds and you are not responsible for their lives. We don't have to make a federal case out of these dreams or somebody else crying. If we are truth oriented, then we cannot deceive ourselves.

Student: On the other hand, as a parent, it appears as if we are responsible for the suffering or whatever of our children. I don't know whether I stifle thoughts of remorse over the mistakes I have made in the past; when these thoughts come up I don't know whether I am stifling these thoughts or healing these thoughts.

Dr. Hora: You are celebrating in a negative way. If we exaggerate the importance of our feelings and emotions we are only celebrating ourselves.

Student: Would that be the same as confirming ourselves?

Dr. Hora: Yes.

Student: I can't seem to go beyond the idea that if somehow I were healthier early on, that perhaps the children would not have to go through unnecessary difficulties.

Dr. Hora: You are a healthy parent. You are helping your children to cope with this crazy life better than without you. Through ignorance we get involved in unnecessary suffering.

Student: He is not responsible. Every parent does the best he or she can at the level that they are at. The children still have to grow up in the human world. They still have to go through the problems. There is very little a parent can do or so it seems.

Dr. Hora: Can you stop the birds from flying over your head?

Student: Children have to experience those things so that they can grow up.

Dr. Hora: It is not necessary but inevitable, right? If you take your emotions seriously, you are going to be enslaved the rest of your life to the thoughts which gave rise to those experiences. Now are we intending to be ruthless and callous? Don't you feel sorry for those little birds? (laughter)

Student: The thought that helps many times is that everything is here to teach us something. We are here to constantly learn so whether it's a dead bird or a dead mouse or mistakes we made with our children or parents, these are all lessons for us to transcend in a spiritual way.

Dr. Hora: We are here for our edification.

Student: And it seems that if we are willing to give up this self-confirmatory element of feeling badly, then somehow something good seems to happen, right? With the example I gave you over the weekend, it seemed had I accepted the thoughts that were present, I would have been stuck with all that. But by being able to turn away, I said there has got to be something better. This can't possibly be my context because there is something else. I was freed of that and it seemed it could have only happened if there was somewhere else to go.

We have some place else to go. So the issue is everything is here for us to learn from.

Dr. Hora: There is a story about Suzuki. He is not a bicyclist. He was a Zen master, a Zen teacher. There were many people dying such as now in the Bosnian involvement, and people were asking him, "What does Zen have to offer us to cope with this horrendous war criminal situation?" It was a terrible situation and he didn't show the slightest concern. He may have said it is regrettable, but he wasn't getting involved in the hysteria of the concern for the tragedies that were happening in every direction. As for the Nazis in World War II, they couldn't say he was an anti-Semite because he wasn't. He was a very healthy individual. More than that, he was an enlightened man. They couldn't get him to join the feelings of sorrow that had affected practically everybody around the globe for what the Germans were doing. People didn't understand how an enlightened man can be so callous. Perhaps the Japanese have a national policy of unconcern with the Jews in Germany, but he tried to explain that these personal reactions are not part of the enlightened life based on reality. How could you explain this to somebody who is involved, right? It is a difficult situation, and it took a long time for students of Zen to understand that emotional reactions are dreams and not reality, and they are not in any way an indication of being virtuous, of being a good man or a bad man or a Nazi or a non-Nazi. He was not involved with the emotionalism and the personal-ism of most people in those days, which was difficult to understand. And slowly, slowly after a few years, we began to see that this is a completely fruitless way of reacting to the situation. Nobody would benefit from the tears of a

Nazi victim. Nothing is beneficial about it, and similarly after a while you can see that everything is a dream no matter how much it hurts, no matter how terrible it is for a human person to see this. It doesn't help, and it is not a virtue to be emotionally affected. We think in terms of emotionalism and we judge people by the depth of their sorrow, and no matter how deep our sorrow is, it has absolutely no value. In psychoanalysis, contrariwise, it was believed that the more sorrow you can feel, the more deeply you can feel the tragedies of human experience, the healthier you are. But unfortunately it doesn't really work that way. Nobody gets enlightened from being sorry or being involved with grief. As a matter of fact, in psychoanalysis they exalted the idea of grief, because the more you experience grief, the idea is that you get healed or you become a better human person because you can cry.

Student: Is regret different?

Dr. Hora: No, nothing personal is desirable.

Student: Regret is also personal?

Dr. Hora: Yes. You neither regret nor not regret. You are living in reality, which is a spiritual universe where there is no messing around with emotions. There is no virtue in that. If you can do something about it, do it.

There was a time when Zen was new and we were reading about these Zen swordsmen, the Samurai. We even saw a movie about them. They would kill each other, these Samurai, at the drop of a hat. They would cut off somebody's head without batting an eyelash. We were all horrified. We asked "How can that be?" After all, Zen is a very noble, spiritual discipline. How can we look at this and say this is right, that these Samurai are right in their activities? So, he said that a Samurai, an authentic Samurai, may have killed a dozen people but he didn't kill them personally. He said that the nature of the Samurai swordsman is that he allows the opponent to impale himself on his sword. Every time it happens, it is a suicide. They had a movie where a Japanese peasant was provoked to dueling with another peasant but the one that was provoked was a Samurai and the other was just a braggart who wanted to show off in the village and he kept nagging him and nagging him and provoked him to come to duel with him and this guy didn't want to duel because he was afraid that this will be the end of this braggart and he tried to explain to him, don't ask me to do that because I don't want you to die. Well this guy showed up in the village and he insisted that they should duel. It took such a long time that the Samurai had to chop wood, and finally he said, "All right, if you insist, but I am warning you, I am a well-trained Samurai." The other guy didn't believe. He was like a braggart. So they got out and faced up against each other and within two seconds the provocateur was dead and this guy didn't do anything. He just held his sword up and he said this is the way that Samurai kill people. They let them impale themselves on the sword. It is unbelievable but that is how it was. So that is the Japanese form of compassion. They allow you to kill yourself.

Student: It sounds like evil destroys itself. You are even watching evil destroy itself.

Dr. Hora: Exactly. That is the whole idea. That is the philosophy of the Zen dualism and the Samurai. But when the Japanese were provoking us in the United States, we took out a longer sword. It was an atomic sword and they got it bad, but that is the way human existence is and that explains the Samurai. Then there were the kamikaze Samurai who believed in committing suicide by piloting the planes directly into a ship. There are various attitudes toward death. So if we see two little birds dead and the mouse and a car battery, we don't have to feel sorry. We just have to understand that these are phenomena, which means they are appearances in which certain thought processes are translated into events. We see the events with our eyes and we take it seriously and we get sick because we don't know how to cope with it.

Student: Is there such a thing as karma?

Dr. Hora: There are millions of Hindus who believe in karma but we are not involved with that. We do not need to speculate about it, because unfortunately there are different theories about it.

Student: Some people are born to be on suicide missions and others are happily living quiet lives.

Dr. Hora: There are those that are living quiet lives? The saying is "lives of quiet desperation." (laughter)

Student: I can see how most of my life has been wasted, worrying or being sad.

Dr. Hora: You are a norm. (laughter)

Student: I can see clearly how we waste our life on worrying about a dead bird or what somebody said to us and it kills all our joy. Seeing that is not enough of a lesson. You forget this lesson and go back to doing the same thing over and over again.

Dr. Hora: If you don't understand what is happening to you that's an unfortunate situation.

Student: I seem to mourn the appearance of a wasted life. How do we really look at that within the context of reality?

Dr. Hora: Every day that we live in ignorance is a wasted life; therefore, we have to hurry up (laughter) and become enlightened and that is what we are working on. One of our friends has gone through about four weeks now of excruciating physical pains in her body and this happened a few years ago to her in the same way. There were excruciating pains in her body, and she was just complaining and complaining and thinking that Metapsychiatry had let her down. Sometimes we go through periods of severe pains until the meaning is clearly understood, and when the meaning has been clearly understood, it sometimes makes us feel that we have been so naive that we are embarrassed to admit it. Yet we cannot get healed until we face up to it openly, quietly, and when it is clearly understood what the issues are, the problem disappears. It can happen to all of us if we are careful about understanding the meaning of our experience.

Student: If we are interested in true freedom, we have to purify our thought processes regarding loved ones. Because if we are humanly in love, then the aspects of hate are inevitable. and if you think that is going to keep you from freedom, it is inevitable to have a death wish. That is all part of that whole context, right?

Dr. Hora: Right.

Student: So if we are truly interested in freedom, in the context of human love, we are not responsible for the other individual. We just have to know that God is available to them as God is available to us when we are moving away from them. So whatever phenomena happen during that process, it is still just a phenomenon in that context. We don't have to be afraid of it. We can see a dead bird. We can see a dead mouse. We can see a dead car. None of that really matters. The only real issue taking place is that we are required to know that we are involved in the human context of love and we need to move to the idea that God's grace is sufficient.

Dr. Hora: Yes. There is a couple in Connecticut and the husband goes from one problem to another-all kinds of problems-financial, emotional and physical and he has a nefarious habit. He would nag his wife all the time, saying: "If only you would change." (laughter) And no matter how many times this occurred, it went on and on and he wouldn't listen to the meanings. He wouldn't consider the possibility of meanings, but insisted that "if only you would change."

Student: You said at the beginning of group that we all seem to have this notion that we can have this unadulterated love affair and we can get it right. Therefore we are involved in operationalism. There is a personal sense in there. Whether it involves a parent or a brother, you have got to get it perfect. We seem to keep working on it, working on it, working on it for years and it doesn't improve. It just has its own life, it seems. So to drop that it's just a question of being loving as you said. Being responsive, that's the best way to be, understanding that love is not something we can do.

Dr. Hora: Love is something we must be careful about. It is very easy to believe that we love somebody, and we are nice people and good and all you have to do is to get the other party to change and then you will be all right. So we suffer from loving people. (laughter) Did you ever consider the fact that human love is an interaction process, so actually it is dangerous to love somebody?

Student: What is a valid way to look at our spouse? (laughter)

Dr. Hora: The best way is gratitude.

Student: For their presence, for their existence.

Dr. Hora: Right. If you can be grateful, then your love is genuine. If it is emotional, it is very dangerous.

Student: How could I tell? What does that mean — emotional?

Dr. Hora: If you are emotional, then you are thinking about how you feel about him or her. It is a feeling issue.

Student: And the idea of gratitude is just appreciative of their existence.

Dr. Hora: You are praising the world for knowing such an individual that can share life. Just praise the Lord.

Student: A sentence jumped out at me from a book I was just ruffling through which said the more cheerfully we can hate our spouse, the better off we are. (laughter) I thought it was very funny because what it said was that we take hatred as well as love so very seriously, and if we can just be cheerful about it and watch it go by, we are better off.

Dr. Hora: And where are we?

Student: Well, we are just not serious about emotions.

Dr. Hora: Seriousness of course is always dangerous. Somebody tells you I am in love. You say to them, get out of here. (laughter)

Student: So is it valid to tell your spouse you love him if you appreciate him? (laughter)

Dr. Hora: It is not recommended. (laughter)

Student: You sound like Dr. Ruth. (laughter)

Student: But hatred particularly has such as emotional impact. Just the word is very frightening to people.

Dr. Hora: Many people are filled with hatred. Of course many people get sick over this. It is not recommended. Neither to love nor hate but to be grateful and remember that God is the only lover. God is the only love. So if we are grateful then love is not personal or impersonal; it's an awareness of God's good and actually that is really freedom.

Student: You are grateful for your parents?

Dr. Hora: You are grateful for whatever good comes to you in your experience, what makes sense, what is intelligent, what is liberating. If we are conscious of being grateful, we have no problems. Grateful people are free people. They don't enslave anybody; neither can they be enslaved by anybody and that is about the best.

4

The Meaning of Attachment

Dr. Hora: Everybody has a chair with his name on it. (laughter) Isn't that something? What is attachment?

Student: Comfort.

Dr. Hora: It's comfort?

Student: Seemingly.

Student: Is that why we sit in the same chair every week, because we are attached to it?

Dr. Hora: You don't ask why.

Student: I thought it was the fear of change, wanting everything to be the same, all the time.

Dr. Hora: Yes, Okay. So it's the same. We get attached to persons, places, things and ideas, right. You see that. That's her chair. (laughter)

Student: We laughed at Archie Bunker. No one was allowed to sit in his chair, ever.

Dr. Hora: Then Meathead came along and put down the right stuff, the right shoe. He broke the rules. This is attachment.

The Buddhists are very much afraid of attachment. They warn people not to get attached to anything ever. What happens when we are attached? You see that it is so widespread. Almost everybody has a tendency to form attachments as if we were made of glue or flypaper or something.

Student: Attachment seems to be a form of wanting and being fearful of not being associated with what we are involved with. Attachment is the fear of loss of that to which we are attached.

Dr. Hora: We are afraid of freedom. Would you believe that? So we are always talking about how great it is to be free. It's a free country. We celebrate the idea of freedom, but when it comes to living freely, it is not so easy. What makes us so fearful of freedom?

Student: I think it means that you would have to be alone. As an individual, you would have to stay solitary in order to be free.

Dr.: Hora: So?

Student: Going back to freedom. It sounds good on paper but it can be very scary to have to be solitary. You know it sounds very nice when you read about it in booklets and stuff.

Student: Do we know what freedom is?

Dr. Hora: Well we could ask the rabbi.

Student: Fear of the unknown?

Dr. Hora: It could be. On the other hand, it could not be.

Student: But isn't it our idea of what we are? Because of the attachment that makes us into what we think we are.

Dr. Hora: Like for instance, what?

Student: Like being president of a board and feeling that gives you a lot of personal satisfaction. So that is an attachment.

Dr. Hora: An attachment to the board?

Student: To the board, to that work.

Dr. Hora: Can we get attached to a board?

Student: Yes, because it gives you personal acclaim and it makes you feel good. Then you are attached to it. At least I feel that I am attached to it.

Dr. Hora: You are just repeating words now. Put it this way. Who needs freedom? What is the big deal about being free? We are so scared of it. Nobody really keeps it in mind. Everybody always goes back to the same spot, to the same thing. We don't want to be free. On the other hand, if we are not free, we complain. Isn't that so?

Student: It seems to have something to do with being able to let go. When you are attached, you are hanging onto something, and if you can let it go you are free.

Dr. Hora: Is that so? There is a story about a philosopher who was a friend of a king and they went on a walk in the garden, and they were talking about this thing that we are talking about now. The king said, "I have no problem with attachments." The philosopher at that point suddenly jumped up into a tree and climbed into the branches and sat there, and the king became annoyed and said, "Come on. Let's continue our lovely walk," and the philosopher said, "I cannot go. The tree won't let me." He got attached to the tree, and he blamed the tree for his being immobilized and imprisoned. We often complain about people who enslave us or force us to stay here and not go there, right? Or they make us eat with the left hand and not the right hand or insist that we have these habits or that we be attached to all kinds of things in every direction. Every one of you is sitting today in the same place that you have been sitting for ages, and there is no freedom to sit somewhere else. Anybody who complains of not being free is ridiculous. Nobody really wants to be free. Everybody wants to be imprisoned by habits.

Student: I don't think they want to be imprisoned by habits. I think we just become like a slave to the habit and the issue is safety. I don't know if it's so much that I want it that way but that I feel scared to do it another way. It frightens me.

Dr. Hora: Yes, okay, so what are you saying? Just because you are scared, then it is all right to be immobilized and to be attached? That's how you explained it.

Student: You said we want to be.

Dr. Hora: Nobody is forcing you to sit there. Nobody is forcing everybody to sit in the same place. But if you say people are scared, what do you mean?

Student: The habit feels safe and it's scary to take another seat.

Dr. Hora: Okay, then it's all right. Then it's all right to be attached in life, because if we are attached in the small things, then it is all right to get attached in big things also. In existential situations, we are attached to a person, to a thing, to a place, or to an idea. Are we attached because we are afraid to be free, or are we afraid to be free because we are attached? Is there anybody in the world who is free? Have you ever known anybody who was free?

There was a TV show. I think it was a Star Trek show where they had a man there who was half white and half black. He was a very interesting fellow, but then after a while another man appeared and he was also half white and half black. People thought these are just brothers or something, but these two guys hated each other with a violent passion and just wanted to murder each other. They couldn't live on the same boat. They would be asked how it is that they hate each other so much because one is half white and half black and the other is half white and half black. "Yes," one explained, "but he is white on the wrong side." That was disturbing for him. Then we have these racial problems, these ethnic problems, wars and fights and all kinds of difficulties in living, and it leaves no flexibility. It's rigidity when we are attached. Everything has to be the same, all the time. If you want to pick your nose, you have to use the same finger. You don't have the freedom to use another finger. It can be absurd. It can go on and on, this human inclination toward forming attachments.

Now the enlightened Buddhist teachers knew about this curse on mankind. They warned their students to be very alert not to fall into the trap of getting attached to anything. It is not easy, but it is important. Why is it important? Sometimes we are attached and we don't realize it, and sometimes we are attached and we think we are not attached. We just love somebody. Attachment can masquerade as love. I love to be close. I love this individual. I love that house. I love this country. We use the word love to cover up the fact that we got ourselves imprisoned through a mental habit of attachment, and we are afraid to be free. Can't you be free while you are attached? There is nothing wrong with the way we are sitting tonight. It is comfortable. We don't realize that we are in a state of attachment right now because we don't have the flexibility to participate in a situation with the slightest change.

Student: Does that mean that we are asleep and wouldn't allow a new idea to come in? Does our survival depend on us being free? Is it that crucial? I mean our actual survival. If we don't learn what freedom is and we don't learn to be free of attachments, is it really dangerous?

Dr. Hora: There are all kinds of dangers. Suppose an event occurs where you are forced to change position or to separate yourself from something that you are attached to? There are all kinds of things happening-political wars, natural disasters. People sometimes have to flee from their homes, right? There are volcanic eruptions, families are broken up, and people have to leave their habitual ways of living. Certain radical changes are forced upon us, and we then are more or less incapable of coping with them, and it is very painful. Whereas, if we would understand freedom, we would not be so incapable. We would be able to cope much better in such situations.

It reminds me of a saying Jesus uttered, "Foxes have holes, birds have nests, but the son of man has no place to lay his head" (Luke 9:58). What did he mean? He wasn't complaining. It sounds like he was complaining. He never really complained. He was always teaching, right? The teacher cannot complain. He has to teach. He is attached to teaching.

(laughter) Even animals get attached. Three or four deer always come to the same place to graze near our house. There is nothing to graze. They don't go to another place. They always come back. They are attached to that particular spot.

Student: How can we live without attachment?

Dr. Hora: That is a good question. Somewhat premature, but first we have to understand the meaning of attachment and then we can ask that question, right?

Student: It seems to me that if the things I am attached to weren't there I would have a great sense of void. That scares me. That void just seems like-

Dr. Hora: Suppose you were attached to a habit of smoking and suddenly you cannot smoke. It is forbidden. Did you see what compulsions, what suffering people go through when their attachment to such a silly little thing, a piece of paper, tobacco and blowing smoke, is taken away? (laughter) They cannot live without it, right? That is attachment. Whatever we attach to is our God. The Bible warns us all the time against idolatry. What is an idol? It is something that becomes unduly important to us, giving us the illusion that our life depends on it, that we couldn't survive without it. Now I ask you, if you would change seats, would you survive a group session? (laughter) We can contemplate the meaning of the human inclination to form attachments.

Student: Some attachments seem more innocuous than others.

Dr. Hora: That's right. You are correct. But we can contemplate exploring the meaning of the human inclination to form attachments.

Student: But it is also like what we cherish, what we hate and what we fear. Many attachments are things that we hate.

Dr. Hora: Sure. A man says I hate this woman tremendously, but I couldn't live without her. (laughter) It is true more often than not. Have you ever heard of this? (laughter)

Student: It seems like our whole identity is based on our attachments. Our whole sense of being and presence is what we are attached to. How can we easily give that up?

Dr. Hora: Nobody is asking you to give it up. All that we are trying to do is understand that we are too religious. The problem is that we are too religious. For some people, religion is another word for an attachment to an idea and to a ritual, to a belief system, to a superstitious preoccupation. We get attached, and to give up an attachment is like dying. So Jesus said again, "Whosoever would lose his life for my sake shall find it" (Matt. 16:25). Freedom he defined as knowing the truth. The truth is God. But I mean the real God, the God above the god, as the saying goes. We can only find freedom when we understand that we are totally, inexplicably, individualized aspects of infinite, divine life. Then our attachment to the real God, not the religious system, but to God, makes it possible to be free. St. Paul said, "I am the prisoner of the Lord" (Eph. 3:1). If we understand what he meant, we would also be free. Because if you understand God, then there is no more need for attachments; you are solidly, securely positioned in reality. "Commit thy ways unto the Lord, and thou shall be established in true freedom" (Prov. 16:3). If we don't understand God, if we don't understand who we are, and what we are and where we are, and what our purpose is, then at best we could become religious, and at worst become fanatical over some nonsense. There are all kinds of groups of people who get attached to an idea, to a system, to a ritual, to a superstition. It can be political or economic or all kinds of things. Whenever you are attached to something, this something becomes your god, and it's always a false god. The real God you cannot get attached to. Isn't that interesting? You can get attached to almost anything in the world — even to the wind. Your own wind or somebody else's. (laughter) You can get attached to that, but it is not possible to get attached to the real God. How is that?

Student: This God is not something we can imagine. It is not dimensional.

Dr. Hora: You could imagine, but it is just imagination.

Student: It still isn't so clear what the meaning is of the inclination to form attachments.

Dr. Hora: The meaning is that we judge by appearances. If we judge by appearances, it would seem to be very important to cling to something, or someone, or some system, or a place or an ideology. Who can live alone? Man cannot survive alone. He has to be integrated with something viable. If we don't understand God in an existentially valid way, then we have no other choice but to reach out to cling to something that is more tangible, something that we can see and feel, touch and fight with.

Student: This could get tricky because in society the world is based on order. So what would be a guideline to check up on yourself? I mean compared with knowing that what one is doing essentially throughout his or her whole life is staying in the same apartment and the same job. You know this type of routine that we set up. How do you know when you are being orderly or when you might be fooling yourself? You can say that this is just the system and I know what I am doing. But how do you wake yourself up?

Dr. Hora: It would seem that if we are not attached to some system, then there would be anarchy and chaos, right? In different periods of time, there are certain trends in our culture where ignorant ideas take hold of people's imagination, and they grab hold of it and wind up in anarchy and chaos. We saw this with the flower children, with all kinds of trends when people were reaching out. There were these cults, religious cults and groupies that always wound up by breaking up and produced a lot of misery, because you cannot replace God. You may have an illusion that there is order. Suppose you are in the Army where there is terrific order-right? It doesn't work, because there is always something going wrong. On the other hand, if you are enlightened about yourself in the context of the valid God, then your order is based on aesthetics and love-intelligence, right usefulness, and everything you do is orderly, intelligent, peaceful, harmonious and beneficial. An enlightened individual doesn't have to be controlled. He has an inner discipline derived from direct awareness of God as infinite Love-Intelligence and that is freedom, and that is peace, and that is spiritual blessedness. It's a whole 'nother smoke.

Student: It seems as though attachment is a form of self-confirmation.

Dr. Hora: It feels like self-preservation. Sure. Freedom is precious, but it is not easily realized.

Student: Let's say you are working on a computer and you are very slow and it's to your advantage to work on a faster computer. The work would get done faster.

Dr. Hora: Because you are in a hurry.

Student: I am always in a hurry.

Dr. Hora: Then you are attached to speed.

Student: Say you are paid by the hour and so they get you a new computer and it's fast and the work gets done much faster. But what has happened is that you get attached.

Dr. Hora: Yes, and after a while you seem very slow. (laughter)

Student: It seems to be better than the old system. It's faster and the work is getting done faster, but yet there is this attachment that has formed.

Dr. Hora: True. It's like getting attached to a girl. She is wonderful, but not for long. (laughter) She seems to be very slow. (laughter) That is what happens with all these attachments. They don't really work.

Student: Can you justify something in terms of it being supposedly more productive?

Dr. Hora: We appreciate productivity, and intelligent efficiency as long as we are not attached to it. As long as our awareness of life and all there is in it, its functions, is based and anchored in God. Because, after all, God is the supreme creative principle of the universe, and whatever there is that is beautiful, good, intelligent, useful, and harmonious is God manifesting in this universe. We can appreciate that, but we do have to know that freedom is a very precious commodity not easily attained and not easily preserved. We can lose it. It is important to appreciate it in its true sense because very often freedom deteriorates into license. For instance, say you want to be free to smoke in the elevator, and you do it and you enjoy it. People are coughing and you enjoy it-right? But how long will that go on? Then you are not fighting for freedom; you are fighting for license, and everywhere we see that people who think they want to be free are really not freedom fighters; they are license seekers. The politician said yes, we will give you freedom for a certain fee. If you pay taxes, this kind of taxes, and that kind of taxes, and social security-we live in a free country. We are hamstrung with a thousand kinds of taxes they use.

About half a year ago they said, "Yes, you have the freedom to practice as a doctor provided you pay us $335 for the license and you spend a certain number of hours in a certain hospital attending a course in child abuse." I have had the freedom for 47 years to be a doctor and now in order to preserve my freedom, I had to go and attend certain stupid lectures about child abuse. (laughter) What did I learn there? I learned that if I agree to having some suspicion that somebody is abusing a child and if I say nothing about it to the police, I can be arrested and put into jail. Isn't that some freedom? You see how freedom can be perverted in a thousand ways. Just like love. Now freedom is spiritual. There is no other kind of freedom. There are just different arrangements, and licenses. You have to pay to get a license. You have to do certain things. Human beings don't know freedom. Only spiritual beings know freedom. Fortunately we are all spiritual beings, and all that is needed is to wake up to this fact and then everything changes.

Student: What was the meaning of man not having a place to lay his head?

Dr. Hora: He doesn't need a place to lay his head. He doesn't have to be somehow implanted in a rigid situation. An animal keeps coming back to the same place, just like people, but the spiritual consciousness doesn't need to be attached to a place. It is free, more free than a bird. Where would Jesus sit if he were in this group? He said when two or three are gathered in my name, I shall be among them. Of course we are more than two or three. Where is he? Where is Jesus Christ, since he promised he will be here? Now the question is, is Jesus here? Can you see him? No. Well does anybody see Jesus?

Student: To the extent we can see the truth we can see.

Dr. Hora: Right, it is not a person. It is a quality of consciousness. That is the Christ. For the second coming he won't need transportation, and he won't need a white horse to come in on triumphantly. It is the advent of the realization of the truth and freedom that is the Christ's second coming, and third coming, and fourth coming. He keeps coming but nobody notices the coming of Jesus because it is not a person but a quality of consciousness, and it keeps coming and it is always there. It is always available for everybody to see and become free, truly free.

Student: Is open mindedness helpful to know freedom?

Dr. Hora: Open mindedness can perceive the true nature of freedom. If we don't have an open mind, we cannot understand freedom because we are not free. The mind is also enslaved. What is the mind attached to? It is attached to thinking, opinions, systems, computers. (laughter) Whenever we have mental attachments, we are not open-minded and we are not free, and we don't learn anything. It is the saddest part of attachments that somebody is attached to certain schools of thoughts or philosophies, or religious dogma. Then he doesn't have the open mind that would enable him to understand reality from a spiritual standpoint and understand freedom. An open mind is very important.

Student: I showed you a cartoon from a Buddhist magazine. It said Zen vacuum cleaner. No attachments. (laughter)

Dr. Hora: Very good.

Student: I raised some of these points in the past about certain morals. For the first five years when I would go in and have some conversations with a teacher, I would get the impression that everyone came from the same kind of moral background so that when I spoke, there was a context that everybody kind of knew. There was an understanding that you didn't have to explain. Now, if you make a simple statement about condoms, or morals, or God, you don't know where the objections are going to come from. There is this looseness, this indefinable-

Dr. Hora: People don't know what it is.

Student: When I say what I say, I feel like I am not in step with the times. I am some kind of an old fogy that still believes in whatever you want to call it, superstition or whatever. It has me kind of doubting, or wondering if I could look for something to sort of lean on.

Dr. Hora: Be attached to.

Student: Maybe that is what it is. Moral looseness, how would this apply to . . .

Dr. Hora: It would help to know what morality means. What is morality?

Student: A kind of a norm that society has set.

Dr. Hora: No that is ethics. Ethics is a psychological standard of behavior. Morality is a religious standard of behavior. We are neither moral nor immoral, but enlightened. We are under the influence of spiritual values and they don't deal with behavior; they deal with seeing. When you see spiritual values as existentially valid, then you will be ethical, and moral, and loving and free and you don't have to worry about what people will think, whether you are an old fogy, or a young fogy. You know what's what. If you ask people, what is this morality? or what is ethics? or what do people talk about? they really don't know. Most people don't know what morality is. Moral values are derived from the Ten Commandments. Ethical values are psychological standards that evolved from social habits in a certain culture. You are not supposed to stab people in the back. That is an ethical value. Ethics and morality are important for unenlightened people to survive in a certain culture and to function. But we transcend these values and this type of thought and we seek to realize spiritual values that give us a transcendent view of life, not on a psychological level, and not on a religious level but in a divine context. That makes us free. Jesus said, "And ye shall know the truth, and the truth shall make you free" (John 8:32). If you are moral, that is nice but that is not freedom. You get constantly pressured. You're ethical. Of course, it's nice from a social standpoint, but that is not freedom. So we have to go higher (99th floor). (laughter)

Student: Is it ethical to cheat on your income tax?

Student: Only if you can get away with it. (laughter)

Dr. Hora: Ethics and morality have no relevance to freedom. They are relevant to more or less harmonious functioning of individuals within a certain social structure. Morality will not give you freedom. Ethics will not give you freedom. They take away your freedom. You have to sacrifice. You have to sacrifice to pay taxes. You have to sacrifice not to lie and not to cheat, not to manipulate, not to hurt people, and not to gossip about people. That is immoral. But freedom and truth and peace and bliss consciousness come to us from an entirely different system of values that we call spiritual values.

5

Abundance

Student: I have a question about being confronted by panhandlers. Sometimes I give them money; sometimes I don't. In either case, I feel, very often, uncomfortable; if I give them money, I am not really benefiting them and if I don't give them money, I am not really benefited. It's not clear how to understand the situation.

Dr. Hora: This question has been raised a few times already, right? What did we say about it?

Student: I remember it was said not to see the person as lacking or imperfect, because we then confirm their apparent infirmity. But it's not that clear to me what would be beneficial. It's not the behavior toward the individual that counts, but how one views them that counts. Yet it seems very difficult not to see them as impaired.

Dr. Hora: Yes. So there is a dilemma. Could Metapsychiatry have something to say about this problem from the standpoint of the individual? The wider problem, of course, is political, social, and economic, but from the standpoint of the individual who is a student of Metapsychiatry, there must be something that one can contribute. As you said, if you give them money, it is not necessarily good, but if you don't give them money, it is not necessarily good either, right? Now, what's the solution? Is there something that a student of Metapsychiatry can give that nobody else can give? What is there?

Student: The way you see the individual.

Dr. Hora: Right.

Student: And if you see this individual, not as a poor, dirty, homeless person, but as a living soul, here for God, just as he is, then it doesn't matter if we give or not give him anything; it's nice to be generous...

Dr. Hora: Okay, we have to see. Metapsychiatry is mostly about seeing. We are learning to see God and God's universe, the universe of mind where there is abundance of love, of wisdom, of everything good. There is abundance. As Jesus said, "I am come that ye might have life and have it more abundantly" (John 10:10). What did he mean? More money, more cars, more girls, more sex? No, the abundance of divine good is all there is. So if you happen to have small change or small bills, you can say, "Thank God, I have this and I can give this," as much as is suitable in the situation. But primarily what we give is a blessing. What is so blessing about what we give. As you said correctly, we acknowledge that everything and everyone is here for God whether they know it or not. This acknowledgement is for us. It reminds us that these individuals are not what they seem to be, that in reality they are perfect, even as the creator is perfect. Now this is difficult, because what we see (with our eyes) has a powerful impact on our thoughts. Nevertheless, and notwithstanding and irregardless (laughter), we have to make an effort to see them in the context of divine mind. And every time we pass by, and something objectionable hits us in the visual field we must immediately remind ourselves of the truth of divine reality, and this thought can have very far reaching consequences. You never know what can happen to any particular individual whom you behold in the light of the truth. So, give whenever you can, money or food, but above all know that the greatest gift that we can bestow on each other is the Prayer of Right Seeing. We all have learned about the Prayer of Right Seeing which was given to us in Hawaii, right? Did you know that?

Student: No.

Dr. Hora: We had a conference in Hawaii; this prayer occurred to us during the conference, and ever since then, individuals all over the world are blessed by students of Metapsychiatry who invariably remind themselves of the Prayer of Right Seeing. Isn't that nice? We can be grateful to these people that they keep us on our toes, and instead of criticizing them, and blaming them, or blaming Mayor Dinkins or Bush or this or that, we give them of our treasure because to understand some of the truth of God and to share it with others is a great gift that we can bestow, and we are not depriving ourselves of anything. On the contrary, we are blessed by blessing. We get blessed by blessing, right? And we get cursed by cursing. Did you know that? So we don't curse, we don't criticize, we don't judge, we don't blame, we just keep blessing and wind up being blessed ourselves.

Student: I have a question regarding this. I was telling Dr. Hora, earlier in private session that about a year ago I saw a film of the life of the tenor Jose Carreras on television. He had just come out of the hospital after a long battle with leukemia, and right on this film, I saw him as ill, or as having been ill and I was struggling the whole time, as Dr. Hora just described. I was going back and forth with this battle in my mind. Then I saw the film again this weekend, and I was very surprised that I was not battling anymore; I just saw that individual as being perfect. Now the first time, I knew what was required but I just couldn't do it and I felt bad. This time, there wasn't any struggle, and what happens when you are in a position like that where the suggestions of the world take hold of your consciousness and you cannot get rid of them and then at another time, you see correctly without trying to? And I was really happy that I could see that this time. But if you are in a position that you can't, it is something of a mystery.

Dr. Hora: What does it take? That is your question. You have to know that you are the richest girl in the whole world; that your father is infinitely wealthy and you have these treasures to give away. Do we understand this treasure? The truth of being in the context of Divine Reality is a treasure which can bless everyone that we look at. Now, unfortunately, people do not know about this. It is a well kept secret. And what do unenlightened people do? They criticize, they find fault, they condemn, they run away.

Student: They feel sorry.

Student: . . . or they give because it makes them feel good or they are bribing God.

Dr. Hora: Yes, there are many ways of going wrong, if we don't understand the great treasure of the prayer of Right Seeing.

We are in a dilemma. We don't know how to be a beneficial presence in the world. As you say, you give them $100.00 and they could go straight into the liquor store and buy a bottle or the drug addicts could get a fix. There are all kinds of people in this condition and it is not really helpful. The material solutions are no solution. But we can give of our spiritual treasures and it will never diminish. There is a story in the bible that occurred at a time when there was a famine in the land. There was a woman who had two sons and they were so poor that she had to sell her sons for a certain amount of food so that they could survive. She sold them into bondage and she was desperate. And as it happens, a rabbi named Elisha was passing by. He stopped at this woman's house and said, "I would like you to make me a little cake, so that I could eat, because I haven't eaten for a long time." And the woman said, "Are you kidding? I am at the bottom of the vessel scraping up some leftover flour to eat myself and give it to my two sons, so that then we could die." They were so poor. And the rabbi said, nevertheless, and notwithstanding and irregardless I want you to make me a piece of bread. And she said, "What should I do?" So she was willing and then she said, "All my vessels are empty; I don't have a drop of oil, nothing." And the rabbi said, "I'll tell you what I'm going to do. You take all your empty vessels that you have, and borrow some more empty vessels from the neighbors, and take one empty vessel in which you have just a few drops of oil in it and start pouring out from this little thing into the empty vessels." So this woman said, "What shall I do with this crazy rabbi? But I'll do it." And she took this vessel and started pouring and as she was pouring the more oil there was and was filling up all the vessels that were in the household. Pretty soon, it was like a river of oil. She sold this oil and that broke the whole spell of hypnotism of starvation. This whole problem was healed. This is in the Bible (2 Kings 4:1–7) I didn't invent it. But it's very interesting because everything from the Bible is an appropriate lesson recorded for our edification. Now what is the lesson in this story? It says that if a crazy rabbi shows up at your door, don't chase him away. No, the rabbi had a spiritual solution. What is the spiritual remedy to lack?

Student: Abundance.

Dr. Hora: Abundance, of course. You see, lack can only exist in the material world. But if you elevate consciousness into the spiritual realm of spiritual divine Love-Intelligence, that lack, which was so impressive to the eyes and to the material viewpoint, disappears and what you have is a condition that gets healed spiritually, and that's the story. He insisted that this woman learn spiritual generosity by making the rabbi a piece of bread. He didn't need the bread, but he was teaching her how to be generous until it hurts. And that's the lesson, that whenever we see lack, homelessness, sickness, misery, we have to replace this picture with a conscious acknowledgement of the truth of divine reality. And if we are sincere and we have studied and learned the Prayer of Right Seeing, solutions occur. And that's the healing. St. Paul says, "We look not upon the things that are seen" (2 Cor. 4:18) or do appear, but we look at the things that are not seen, you see, and when we are able to look at the things that are not seen, surprising things can and do happen in proportion to our ability to pray in this fashion.

Student: I wanted to ask a question regarding the issue of
giving to people. There is a story in the Bible of the apostles,
where a man is asking for money, and he says, "Silver and gold
I have none, but such as I have I give to thee" (Acts 3:6) and
he heals him. But nowadays when we are not at that spiritual
level, when you say to behold somebody in the context of love,
I notice sometimes that a hidden thought of doubt remains,
and I wonder if it is doing any good because you see people
in very desperate shape, even within the family. I must say
I have some doubts because I am not able to transform the
situation like the apostles did.

Dr. Hora: Well, this reminds me of the lesson that Jesus gave
to some of his students. He said that anything can happen
with prayer; for instance, if you pray believing that all is possible to God and you will say to this mountain, "Get thee
hence and move into the midst of the sea or into yonder
place" (Matt.17:20), as the Bible says, and if you pray believing that this is possible, it will happen. So there was a guy
among his disciples and he said, "All right I am going to pray
hard," and all night he prayed about this mountain because it
was blocking his view and he wanted this mountain to move
away and he prayed and prayed all night and in the morning
he looked out and the mountain was still there, and he said,
"I knew it, I knew it wouldn't work." That's the problem with
doubt. Now, what is the lesson in this? After all, it is normal
to doubt. Of course, Jesus made a mistake in this lesson. He
told the people that what they have to do is to believe. If
you believe in God, in the truth, in what we are saying here,
it won't help at all. What is needed is right knowing, and
that takes a little time and work. Because when you believe

something, you doubt. It is not possible to believe without doubting. So this whole thing is a mistake. Many formal religions are constantly encouraging people to believe: believe in God, believe in Jesus Christ, believe in this, believe in that and the more you believe the more you doubt. You cannot have a coin with only one side. What is needed is, knowing based on spiritual realization. So we study, we read, we meditate, and little by little we begin to realize that there is such a thing as spiritual reality. So when we pray we endeavor to acknowledge spiritual reality. We don't work on believing in spiritual reality. We don't believe in God. We don't believe in Jesus Christ. The hopelessness of formal religions, where people are trying to believe, is getting them nowhere. What is needed is the knowledge that is based on progressive spiritual realization and then good things can happen. There is a tremendous difference.

Student: But between believing where there is doubt and really knowing, what can we do to gain that understanding?

Dr. Hora: You must be interested in realizing this truth. So you don't piddle around with maybe I will see. Let's try this or that. No, you work. This is called contemplative meditation where a certain truth is presented to you either from the Bible or a teacher or from the *Daily News*, and you take this truth and contemplate it with a sincere desire to realize it, to understand it, and it will happen. Little by little, here a little, there a little, we will realize more and more of the truth of divine reality in which we live and move and have our being. And that's the way to go. Everything else is conditional and God says, "You cannot piddle around with me. I need total commitment." And that is what is required.

Student: If you give, wanting to help, it's no good. It won't work because wanting is personal. In other words, if you say there is this homeless person and if I give him money I'm going to help him or maybe I'm not going to help him . . .

Dr. Hora: No, we are discouraged here from wanting or not wanting, but we are encouraged to be interested in progressively realizing divine reality and its power to help us see that what we ordinarily see is not so. Only the unseen is real. The seen is phenomenal; it is a phenomenon. So we are infinitely rich and we don't know it. Imagine you had a million dollars in the Chemical Bank down the street and you didn't know about it. You could be among the homeless, starving on the street, just because you didn't know. That's the way it is with enlightenment. We don't know and we always suffer from not knowing. And every little bit of knowing helps.

Student: Is commitment a progressive interest also? It is not just a one instant happening?

Dr. Hora: Well it is a constant attitude, a desirable attitude where we are interested in realizing the truth of being, of divine reality. And the more often we see that certain healings happen, certain good things happen, the more encouraged we become and the more sincere our commitment becomes, and little by little, we get there.

Student: So commitment, in a way, is being drawn?

Dr. Hora: Well let us put it this way, in being sincerely interested.

Student: When we are asked for something or we are asked to be helpful, do we need to recognize it as not a personal thing that we're doing, but what God wants?

Dr. Hora: Not necessarily. Suppose your children ask, "Let's go to JB Schwartz (laughter as he is corrected to FAO Schwartz) or to the mall." (laughter)

Student: In a helpful sense, what I was talking about earlier, about people in Russia needing food, the helpfulness comes through in right seeing more than it does in the physical manifestation. The coin or the money or the food is just a physical manifestation of what God . . .

Dr. Hora: Yes, and it is just temporary. It quickly fizzles out and it is not very helpful. It is better than nothing, but we have the great blessing of knowing how to give of our secret treasures. And these secret treasures are spiritual. What makes them secret? The Bible says, "It's hid with Christ in God" (Col. 3:1). That which is hidden is a secret, right? What makes it secret? We have secret treasures and we can give them away. What is not known but knowable is a secret. Yes, "He that dwelleth in the secret place of the most high shall abide under the shadow of the almighty" (Ps. 91:1). The Bible speaks about secrets, but not about secretiveness. It's all right to know that there are secrets that must be known but secretiveness is an extremely selfish attitude and it is not helpful. Suppose you are a student who says, "Well, I know the Prayer of Right Seeing and I know that it is very helpful, but I don't want to give it away. I'll keep it to myself. I won't let anybody in on it, right?" Or, "I have this book titled *Beyond the Dream*. It's a nice book. I won't let anybody see it." There are such people. Or I don't want anybody to see it, because they may think I am crazy for reading such a book. There are all kinds of possibilities. In the spiritual realm, the more we treasure something, the more we are willing to give it away. It is easy to be generous, because the more you give it away the more you have it.

Student: Dr. Hora, I don't understand the point about the secret place of the most high. Why is it necessary that the place be secret?

Dr. Hora: Because nobody knows it. And then, of course, let's take the Prayer of Right Seeing. You have to pray it in secret. If you would tell somebody, I'm going to tell you something. I will pray this prayer for you. "Everything and everyone is here for God whether they know it or not." You gave away the secret. There is no secret anymore and the recipient rejects it. You cannot give it away openly. It has to be conveyed on another channel. And that is the value of the secret place of the most high. Where is this place?

Student: In consciousness.

Dr. Hora: In consciousness, right. Who knows about consciousness? What the heck is it?

Student: Could it be awareness?

Dr. Hora: Awareness is the function of consciousness. But certain truths cannot be communicated verbally or openly; they are communicated secretly. Not because we are secretive, but because speaking openly about it is not appreciated. It sounds trite.

Student: And it loses its impact.

Dr. Hora: Yes, sure.

Student: Sometimes, when I am sitting quietly, someone will come to mind, like my mother. It's not that she called on the telephone but a thought of her comes to mind, and it occurs to me, as a blessing. Now is that unsolicited? I mean, is that appropriate?

Dr. Hora: It is appropriate for a daughter to bless her mother every time that she asks for it. And if the thought comes to you, most likely she is asking you to pray for her. It's like an outstretched hand.

Student: Would someone like Jesus have seen everybody the same way though? Would he have had the dimension of thoughts of individuals coming to him or was he on a level where he was a non-personal blessing and it would depend more on his receptivity than on his thought?

Dr. Hora: Well, let's put it this way. Your question is not sufficiently clear.

Student: Well, when the student asked about her mother, you said that we reach a point where we do not think of persons anymore. So when we reach a level of enlightenment would persons come to your consciousness anymore?

Dr. Hora: It is important to lose interest in seeing persons, in being persons, in talking about persons, in greeting persons, and acting as if there really were persons in the world. They seem to be, but we don't have to accept that. We have to know that there are only individual divine consciousnesses. Now every individual divine consciousness is unique, with unique endowments, talent, and gifts and possibilities because God is infinite mind and infinite creator. He creates an infinite variety of reflections of himself. Think of a maple tree in full leaf. It has millions of leaves and every leaf is a maple leaf but every maple leaf is different from every other maple leaf. Isn't that amazing? Now, there's a meaning to this, right? There must be. The Bible says, "And the leaves of the tree are for the healing of the Nations" (Rev. 22:2). What does that mean?

Student: No interaction between them.

Dr. Hora: No interaction between them.

Student: They all receive their life from the tree.

Dr. Hora: Yes, right. In other words, you don't just take the leaves and take it to the pharmacist and have him make a powder out of it to take it in. That's not what is meant, right? Now there are primitive cultures where they use leaves as boons. They believe that this will facilitate the healing, but that's not what the Bible is talking about. The right understanding of the symbolic message in the leaves of a tree says that, just like there is an infinite variety of leaves, there is also an infinite variety of divine ideas and the understanding of this has a healing effect on your way of seeing life. The leaves on a tree co-exist harmoniously. They have no relationship with each other. Did you know that? And that's nice. So we learn from every little thing that comes up. We can learn more and more to know divine reality. The leaves of the tree are for the healing of nations. Nations could live peacefully together and harmoniously if the message about the leaves of the tree is understood. There would be no wars, neither crime, nor revolutions, nor any kind of complications. As Jesus put it, "If thine eye be single, thy whole body shall be full of light" (Matt. 6:22). What did he mean by that?

Student: A focus on the awareness of right seeing?

Dr. Hora: Right seeing, yes. If thy eye is single, it means that in your viewpoint on life there is no interaction thinking, because in order for interaction thinking to happen there has to be double vision. There has to be self and other. So the leaves on the tree do not interact. They just co-exist harmoniously with each other. So the leaves have the single eye. We can have the single eye too, by understanding these symbolic messages from the Bible. Now what happens to relationships between boys and girls if there is no interaction? How is that possible? Would an enlightened boy have a girlfriend? Or would an enlightened girlfriend have a boyfriend? How can one be in such a situation without interaction? How can there be sex without interaction? That's an interesting question. After all, the sexual act in itself appears to be eminently interactive. The boy is doing something to the girl. And the girl calls the police and says... (laughter) "sexual harassment." Consider all these complications of life, nowadays particularly, between men and women. All the difficulties which go on are based on the assumption that there is no possibility of living without interaction; neither between friends, nor between the sexes, nor in families. It is incomprehensible. How can one have sex without interaction thinking? How do the leaves have sex? (laughter) What do the words "harmonious co-existence" mean? It means that nobody is doing anything to anybody and yet there must be sex. How can there be sex without somebody doing something to somebody?

Student: Artificial insemination? (laughter)

Dr. Hora: Doctors are doing something. Now some years ago, I read a treatise about the Buddha's idea of ideal sex: the method of sexual intercourse in Buddhism, notably enlightened Buddhism. First of all, the surprising thing was that it isn't happening in bed. It happens on the floor where a man and a woman sit cross-legged facing each other and they are very good at sitting cross-legged. (laughter) We cannot do this very well, but they can do it, and gradually they come together. And in this process there is a complete joining at the genitals. The man doesn't do it. The woman doesn't do it. Spontaneously the sexual urge does it. So you cannot say that the man does something to the woman or that the woman is doing something to the man. It happens in a most harmonious, gentle and loving way. It is a coming together on both parts, spontaneously, and peacefully and according to the description, most satisfactorily. But it is not a situation where somebody is doing something to someone. And the two are not interacting; they are jointly participating in love. Love is expressing itself in this kind of joining. I thought then that it was extremely beautiful and I still think so. It is the possibility of sexual intercourse without interaction. But you have to learn how to sit (laughter) cross-legged comfortably, without effort, and let it take place by itself, because the power of love will express itself in a joint participation in the good of God. You remember that this is our definition of marriage. This is an interesting aside.

6

What Yen Hui Understood

Student: Dr. Hora, a while ago you mentioned that there is no man without God and no God without man. I've been reading a lot of physics and archaeological things. What is man? It's not the person or the specific people. Historically there was a time where there was not man. There was the cosmos, and there were dinosaurs but there was no man. Is there something erroneous here, because if there is no man, then there is no God in that environment or is that too much science? (laughter)

Dr. Hora: Ordinarily when we speak about man we have an image of a three-dimensional object moving in space. This is the common view of man; so we are used to thinking this way. But if you enter into a deeper understanding of reality, of life, then you see that this is a fiction. There is no such thing as three-dimensional reality. Man is a divine consciousness, a quality. He is not the way he seems to be. The Zen master says "Nothing is the way it seems to be, but neither is it otherwise."

Student: So everything that seems to be, whether it is dinosaurs or appearances, is a projection of...

Dr. Hora: They appear and they disappear. Right? The real man never disappears once he has appeared. Anyone who has seen the real man knows that this man is immortal and immutable. So we are what God is. Nobody has seen God either. And we are the image and likeness of something that nobody has seen. Moses claimed that he saw God. The problem is that we judge by appearances and out of that we arrive at all kinds of mistaken ideas about ourselves and about others. So if we are heading towards enlightenment, we have to learn to see that there is nothing to see. Man is a divine consciousness. That's what the real man is. He is a spiritual being and the visible things of this universe are symbolic structures indicating in what direction our cognition has to evolve. If you observe life from the standpoint of educational levels, you can see that the more primitive we are, the more unenlightened we are, the more we cherish and hold on to and imagine the tangible, the material, the mortal, the things that have form or are formless. The Zen master issued this interesting saying: "Form is formlessness and formlessness is form." Everybody is puzzled about that. What in the world could that mean?

Student: Well, that which we see that has form is really non-existent; what we don't see is what really is . . .

Dr. Hora: Not so. Just because we cannot see something doesn't qualify it as real. There is such a thing as error. The human individual is given the difficult task of coming to know himself or herself the right way. There was a famous rabbi, a Talmudist, and he said to his disciples, "I was going to write a book about man, but then I changed my mind. I thought it better if I don't." He could have gotten crucified in those days. He was a wise rabbi.

Student: You say the visible is a symbolic structure, like, let's say, going to work. You see people, their external, seemingly three-dimensional images. How are those symbolic?

Dr. Hora: Well have you ever seen God going to work? The Bible says, "The Father worketh hitherto and I work" (John 5:17). and, "The Father that dwelleth in me, he doeth the works" (John 14:10). Then, man is a symbolic structure pointing in the direction of a certain existence that has the quality of working. So we are symbolic structures for God. We are what God is. And the Zen Master says, "The finger is not the moon," and the menu is not the food. (chuckle) And the dimensional appearance called man is not God; it is a symbolic pointer in the direction of God. Now people ask, why do we need people? Why does God need people? He's omnipotent, ever present, and knows everything. Why do we need people?

Student: It's lonely at the top.

Dr. Hora: Theologians say that God was lonely so he made Adam and Eve and a snake to have entertainment. That's looking from the wrong end of the binoculars. No. We know God through understanding man. If we understand ourselves in a valid way we come to know God. So God needs us. "This is Life eternal that they may know thee the only true God and Jesus Christ whom thou hast sent" (John 17:3). God seems to want to be known, and man serves that purpose.

Student: And we see each other until we don't need to see anymore, is that it?

Dr. Hora: We see God in each one of us. We are each a symbolic structure for God and the right seeing reveals God to us. And apparently it is very important to God that he may be understood and may be seen correctly. Indeed, we can say wonderful things can happen to anyone who approaches this correctly and gains a more precise and valid understanding of what God is.

Student: Dr. Hora, is that similar to the Yen Hui story?

Dr. Hora: Yes. Do you all know the Yen Hui story? No? Now we will ask the student to explain the Yen Hui story.

Student: There was a man by the name of Yen Hui. He was asked to become an advisor by an Emperor who had a bad habit of chopping off the heads of his hired help if they gave wrong advice. Thus he was very afraid of doing that job. So he went to the Zen master and he told him about his dilemma. And the Zen master said, "You will have to practice mind fasting for three years."

Dr. Hora: A short course in Metapsychiatry.

Student: So he said, this is the part I was trying to recall, "If you see with your eyes..."

Dr. Hora: He asked his teacher, "What is this mind fasting that you are telling me about?" He proceeded to explain what it is. Go ahead.

Student: "If you see with your eyes, don't look with your eyes; if you hear with your ears, don't listen with your ears; if you think or understand with your mind, don't think or understand with your mind, but learn to see, hear and understand with the Spirit."

Dr. Hora: Isn't that simple?

Student: No. So he practiced that and . . .

Dr. Hora: He practiced that for three years and then he came back to his teacher and said, "Master, I think I have become enlightened." So the Master said, "Prove it to me." So what did he say?

Student: He said, "Before I practiced mind fasting I knew that I was Yen Hui, but now that I have practiced mind fasting, I know there never was a Yen Hui."

Dr. Hora: So what happened to Yen Hui?

Student: Well, maybe that's what we were talking about, that he realized who he really was and then there was no more person.

Dr. Hora: Right. Did you all hear this? He discovered his true identity. Previously he thought he was just an ordinary guy, a highly educated mind, a philosopher who was appointed to the court of the Emperor. He was afraid to accept the job, and when, after practicing mind fasting he said this to the teacher the teacher said, "Yes, you have attained enlightenment and you can safely assume this position." What made it safe?

Student: He didn't exist.

Dr. Hora: He didn't say he didn't exist. No. He knew the truth of his being. Therefore, he would not provoke the Emperor to be mad at him or be jealous of him or to argue with him. The Emperor would appreciate the wisdom coming from his enlightened consciousness, and that's the way to be safe, not only in China, but also in New York, even though it is a little more difficult here. You just call a taxi and start a conversation with a taxi driver and pretty soon you get your head chopped off. Yes. Yen Hui is a beautiful story of what happens to someone who becomes enlightened and how it is that someone gets enlightened. You have to learn not to hear with your ears, not to see with your eyes, and not to understand with your mind or intellect. What is that? There is the great void.

Student: Collectively, these things are saying, "Don't judge by appearances."

Dr. Hora: Yes, and don't imagine that you can think, and that you have a mind of your own. The Bible says, "It is the spirit that quickeneth; the flesh profiteth nothing" (John 6:63). When we are unenlightened, we are used to judging by appearances, imagining that we are hearing something that nobody said, or we are seeing something or figuring something out. None of these things are really happening. It is the spirit that is life and the spirit is in us, and then we are alive and then there is wisdom and freedom and harmony and beauty and PAGL (peace, assurance, gratitude, love). Everybody longs for it. People study spirituality in many forms everywhere throughout the world, and it has always been that way. But somehow it never hits the mark. It's all there, and people study in every language, in every tradition, in every religion. People seek enlightenment.

Student: What's the meaning of the fact that we never hit the mark?

Dr. Hora: We are usually too attached to our husbands or spouses. And they mislead us . . . with cockamamie ideas. (laughter)

Student: It's a beautiful thought that that's what we are all looking for — God. Is everybody looking for God?

Dr. Hora: Everybody without exception is looking for God; there is nothing else to look for.

Student: They just don't know where to look. I was talking to an individual this week, who is very talented and very creative, but is constantly looking and doing things without any fulfillment. You can see the searching and doing many wonderful individual works and briefly enjoying a pleasure filled life. But always a sense of emptiness comes through. It occurred to me that this individual is really looking.

Dr. Hora: Sure.

Student: Dr. Hora, most people seem to think they are empty; yet we're told here that they are fulfilled already. What's the mistake? Are we supposed to meditate on the fact that we are already fulfilled in God, and don't have to look for something. It seems to be a big mistake, this looking for something. Yet we're being told it's already present. Is that all it takes...

Dr. Hora: Who told you that we are already fulfilled?

Student: I thought we said we are already the sons of God.

Dr. Hora: Yes, but we don't know that. Jesus said, "Blessed are they that hunger and thirst after righteousness [right understanding] for they shall be filled" (Matt. 5:6). So we are not fulfilled until we have reached the right understanding. You hear some people in religious circles saying that we are already enlightened. There is nothing to do, so let's go have a pastrami sandwich. Now, we live in ignorance, and we suffer the consequences continuously. This is purgatory. This life is purgatory. Do you know what purgatory is?

Student: Hell. It's between heaven and hell.

Dr. Hora: You know the geography? The word purgatory — where does it come from?

Student: To purge.

Dr. Hora: Yes. What are we purging?

Student: Ignorance.

Dr. Hora: Ignorance. We are full of ignorant ideas and we share them generously. Wherever you look, people share their ignorance with each other, having a good time about it.

Student: This story of Yen Hui puzzles me. If you are unenlightened and you haven't studied any spiritual teaching, you just see people as they appear to be. Then we're told that instead of seeing the person, the physical manifestation, we must look to see spiritual qualities in the individual and that we can practice seeing spiritual qualities. But that doesn't seem to be anywhere near what Yen Hui discovered. Is it possible to tell anyone what it was that he really saw other than to say?

Dr. Hora: You could ask, "What is it about mind fasting that would precipitate you into enlightenment?" Isn't that what you want to know? What is it about mind fasting that would bring about your enlightenment?

Student: Basically, I don't know the answer, but last week we talked about making a radical stand against fantasies. We could start with that. And every time that tape starts spinning, the ignorant tape, we can see it, and we have the God given ability to turn to a valid principle. And if that's mind fasting then perhaps that is how we discover the void or what is that we're turning to. If we continue with that, maybe we break through to something.

Dr. Hora: What we have said about Yen Hui and the practice of mind fasting was not all we could say on the subject. Yen Hui was a long time student of this famous Chinese teacher called Chuang Tsu. When he came to Chuang Tsu, he was already recognized as a great philosopher and was known among the intelligentsia, so he was better able to make use of this discipline of mind fasting than anybody else. He was so sincere that he withdrew from the world for three years and studied day and night. I suppose he started something like this. Every morning he would wake up and say, "I am not this body. I am not this person. I am not what people call me, Yen Hui. Everything I see and everything I was told about myself seems true, but it is not true."

It is very helpful to deny the appearance world, and work from the negative up to the positive. And in the process, when you hear a bird singing, ask yourself, do I hear this, or is my ear hearing this? If you see a snake coming toward you, you say am I seeing this or am I just imagining this? You question every thing about yourself that you have always taken for granted. Gradually you reach a point where you annihilate your sense of self and you are more and more in the void that they call emptiness. Then gradually you begin to see that you are something other than what you have believed yourself to be. So when you hear with your ears, don't think that it is the ears that hear. Beethoven could hear a symphony while he was deaf. So with this discipline, with great understanding Yen Hui reached a point where he could say that he always thought that he was Yen Hui, but now he could see that there never was a Yen Hui. So then you ask him, "If there never was a Yen Hui, what was there? Can you touch him? Can you punch him? Can you kill him? Can you love him?"

What is this great mystery of identity? So he took a trip to Texas and they explained to him that "You ain't never was nothing" and that brought a big laugh. But he became free; we call it, liberated. So next time you're getting a haircut, and the barber asks, "Mister, are you something?" you will know what to say. That's what we get from Metapsychiatry. There is an interesting theory that is occurring now. We ask how come some people have a sense of humor and some people don't. What is this great gift? No other life form has it except us. It seems that in order to be able to laugh, we have to be able to endure the idea of our own nothingness. Because if you see an individual who has no sense of humor, what do you see right away? He takes himself seriously. He has no sense of humor. What does it mean if we take ourselves seriously? It means that we think that we are somebody, right? At that point we are dead, because an individual who cannot laugh is really dead. Maybe comedians are closer to enlightenment than they realize. I remember Jack Benny. He was always laughing at himself in a sort of charming way. He was a wonderful comedian.

Student: There was Bob Hope with his wonderful longevity.

Dr. Hora: Yes. If you see a serious man keep away from him. I remember as a young professional I would attend yearly conferences of the psychoanalytic society and what struck me was that nobody had a sense of humor there. Everybody walked around with an air of great importance and thought that they all were very serious people who imagined that they had more knowledge in their heads than anybody else in the world. It was so boring. I wasted those years studying their stuff and looking up at the imposters, ignoramuses and very serious people. "For the earth shall be filled with the knowledge of the Lord as the waters cover the sea" (Isa. 11:9). This is the good future.

Student: I always wondered why I like the sea so much. Now I know.

Dr. Hora: Yes, you have described how much you like the ocean, the water.

Student: Dr. Hora, how can we not take mind fasting seriously?

Dr. Hora: If you take mind fasting seriously, you will never accomplish it. It's a gift of God. It's a gift of self-transcendence. It's from God. We are able to rise above our customary ways of thinking. So you say, I am not this body and I am not this brain. I am not this intelligence: I am not my eyes or my ears. All are symbolic structures pointing beyond themselves. And then you can laugh. Don't take yourself seriously, for heaven's sake.

Student: Actually, that sounds very liberating.

Dr. Hora: Sure, sure.

Student: It reminds me of what I read by the writer William Faulkner. In his fiction, one of his techniques consists of saying it's not this, it's not that, and so on and so on until finally saying what it is: some quality or affect of character. He goes through all these negatives to reach a positive.

Dr. Hora: This is called *via negativa,* the negative approach to the study of reality. It's very good.

Student: So, it isn't possible to really understand something unless we go through this negative process so that we can see what it is that is not. Is that right?

Dr. Hora: Well, you cannot jump at Faulkner's idea and that of a few other people as a foolproof technique of attaining enlightenment. It is just interesting to hear how some people seek to understand more of the truth. So it's not bad for you to wake up in the morning and to look around and to ask yourself, "Who is this person in bed, now; is he my husband or is it a stranger?" (laughter) So you start by asking, "Is this me, etc.?" And if this seems too simple for you, you can ask, "Who are you? Who is he?"

Student: I was thinking about what you said about symbolic structure. I find myself wanting and thinking about having a dog again and I can almost fantasize a dog, whether it would be right to get one?

Dr. Hora: Dogs are highly recommended, except the rabbis don't like dogs. I once lived in another building on Central Park West and in that building was a great rabbi of a nearby synagogue. I had a dog at that time, a beautiful white poodle. The rabbi seemed to abhor him. He said, "Don't come close with him; this is a *kelev.*" You know what a *kelev* is? That's a Hebrew name for a dog. He had an aversion to dogs. And that dog was so sweet, so bright, so full of life. I loved him very much. So don't worry. If you can get a dog and are able to care for him, by all means do so. They are wonderful companions, and they bring out all the love in you, whatever is left yet. (laughter)

Student: But I'm thinking, though, that maybe I am trying to substitute something.

Dr. Hora: Well, it is worthwhile. You've had dogs before, so you know how it is to have a dog. You have to take him out. (laughter) It is a great urinary responsibility. (laughter)

Student: Well we had a different life style then. So I guess what I get concerned about is that part of it, the affection, is just something about it that seems loving. But it's questionable, as you say, if I'm ready to undertake the responsibility. Do I get involved like that again with the caring?

Dr. Hora: First you have to buy him a license and then you have to buy him a country estate, surrounded with a fence, so it will be easy to take care of him. If he wants to go out, you just let him go. That's a nice way to have a dog. But if you have to take him in the city, and let him smell everything, you can get tired of that. And then there's the pooper scooper (laughter), the law of the city, right?

Student: I heard a wonderful comment about people who have an urge to have dogs. On my way to work, I walk past a pet store and it's enough to break your heart. Every time you want them all. And someone said, well there are two phenomena: one is getting the dog and that's where you pick out the animal and there is all that great excitement and you bring it home and have all the initial enthusiasm, and then there's having the dog, and having the dog is three walks a day, seven days a week for the foreseeable future.

Dr. Hora: It's important to have the space.

Student: I was trying to understand if I was trying to substitute something. By wanting or having this urge for a dog, I wondered if it was really about something else. I am trying to substitute with a dimensional thing as opposed to maybe there is something else that needs to be...

Dr. Hora: There was an American poet who lived in Paris who said, "A rose is a rose is a rose." And we can say a dog is a dog is not a substitute is a dog. And they are all adorable, wonderful creatures. So don't speculate that it is a substitute for mother or for somebody else. It's a dog. You love a dog because it is very affectionate. So if you can manage to care for a dog it is wonderful to have one. It's the same with baby children, you know, but you cannot return the child to the store.

Student: Is what we are talking about, loving to be loving? I mean, that's the challenge for a love object, and taking care of it. Think we ought to get a dog? (laughter)

Student: I found that when we had an opportunity to purchase a dog that was already trained, I didn't do it. But when I let it go and didn't follow through, I felt heart-broken. But again I noticed that emotionalism, and what was that all about? Feeling that way about feeling something...may not be kosher.

Dr. Hora: Well, it is human affection; it is always good and bad. Attachments develop.

Student: It was as if I was becoming attached to the entity of it.

Dr. Hora: I saw a film where a middle-aged man came to a prostitute and they were talking it over, and he said, "My wife treats me like a dog." And the prostitute said, "Well, I can do that to you anytime." So they made an arrangement that once a week he would visit her. And she said, "I even have a choking collar. And we can start by learning to heel." So they made an agreement, but this man was so accustomed from childhood on to be treated as a dog, that he longed to have this experience. Many of the perversions that people display are just desires to relive certain abusive experiences from childhood. What was interesting was that in this film the director understood the dynamics of the situation. It was a very helpful prostitute; I can do this for you right away, treat you like a dog. There are people who have a desire to be maltreated because in their childhood they were mistreated. It is a very tragic aspect of the human condition that we can desire pain and humiliation and abuse, because somewhere in the memory bank there is a remembrance of the experience, which was extremely self-confirmatory. You see, when a child is abused, beaten, tortured, or humiliated, he feels pain, but he also feels important. Nothing is worse than being ignored. So if you have no choice you choose abuse; it's better than being ignored. This is the dynamic of the tragedy we hear about, of so many women, children, and people who are abused in their childhood. The trouble with that is that you fall in love with the experience and then you attract it to yourself. "Nothing comes into experience uninvited." So we can invite disasters, sicknesses, maltreatments, abuses, all kinds of what are called perversions in order to re-experience that childhood experience. And the rationalization is that maybe such repetition would help you to overcome it. But you never overcome it. The only way to overcome it is to know that we are not that person. When you understand the Yen Hui story, then all the invalid ideas of abuse of the past are erased, because you are not that individual. You are free of that conditioning. It is very sad when a child gets abused, because he is being conditioned for that experience.

7

Koans and the Rosetta Stone
of Metapsychiatry

Student: Yesterday we were talking with you about the parable of the shepherd who had 100 sheep and one was lost. He left the 99 to go out and find the one that was lost. I wondered if you would discuss that some more. I pondered it today and I don't believe I know the full implications of that parable.

Dr. Hora: Who knows the parable of the lost sheep? (Matt. 18:12–14).

Student: Jesus described how if there is a flock of 100 sheep and one of them gets lost, the shepherd will leave the 99 and find the one that is lost.

Dr. Hora: This was on television yesterday and we were watching it. A man who was a member of the church told the story that the shepherd went after the one sheep that was lost to look for him. The man said this was very stupid to do because in the meanwhile he could have lost the 99 other sheep, right? That would be logical and reasonable for a human shepherd. How can he take care of all the 99 sheep and go after the one that was lost? The Bible says that he did that and he found the sheep, put him on his shoulder and he brought him back to the flock and there was great rejoicing, right? So what good is such a stupid parable? If you are a normal, human person you will say, "This is a stupid story." It has no relevancy to anything. Now, does the Bible have stupid stories? Well, there are all kinds of stories, but it is good to understand them. Does anybody understand this story? Nobody dares to understand it?

Student: Is this where the misconception came, that from the religious point of view we are supposed to go out and save the one that is lost?

Dr. Hora: Yes, of course. So is the Bible teaching us how to be a stupid shepherd? It doesn't make sense if you have 99 sheep, to turn your back on them and go after the one that was lost.

Student: Wasn't the implication that the 99 were safe?

Dr. Hora: No, he didn't say that. They didn't run away. It's a mystery why they didn't because if it is a stupid story then they would probably get scattered.

Student: I think it's wonderful imagery in the sense that if we recognize God as our shepherd, our director, and if we are lost, meaning that we are separated from God, reality is such that we will be found, that we will eventually be directed back to-

Dr. Hora: How do you know that? Isn't that just a theory? There are these 99 sheep and he goes off looking for the 100th.

Student: In reality none of us are separated from God. It just appears that way.

Dr. Hora: In reality. What do you mean?

Student: In reality there is no such thing as being separated.

Dr. Hora: Your little doggie. Suppose he runs away.

Student: He did, by the way.

Dr. Hora: He did?

Student: A couple of days ago and there was a reason for it.

Dr. Hora: Did he come back?

Student: Yes, wagging his tail.

Dr. Hora: That's an enlightened dog.

Student: He was hungry. (laughter)

Dr. Hora: There were two professors of theology. They were talking about this parable and they were giving each other very complicated explanations and the more they talked about it, the clearer it became that they didn't understand it at all. Theology will not help us to understand the Bible. It is very interesting.

Student: When you hear two people talking like that or some of the comments that were made here, how do you know what the parable is really about?

Dr. Hora: That's a good question.

Student: That happens all the time. There are so many different things that we can point to and then you can wonder, what is the real meaning of it, and how come it's this and it isn't that and how do we know that this is the meaning and other things aren't the meaning?

Dr. Hora: Do you have any answers?

Student: To that question, no.

Dr. Hora: Anybody?

Student: Would it helpful to give an example of this problem?

Dr. Hora: Yes.

Student: We had a business situation where we found out yesterday that we were being sued because a man fell off a scaffold at the job site where we have construction supervisors. He is suing everyone involved — all contractors involved — and since we decided to go out of business about a year ago, our insurance is in question. I am not sure whether we didn't renew it at the same rate, or if we didn't renew it at all and therefore we do not have the proper coverage. He is suing for millions of dollars and it is a frightening thing when you consider it in human terms where you could be faced with the loss of everything. So when I presented it to Dr. Hora, he repeated this parable that we just heard and in this context what I understood was that in divine reality these astronomical numbers don't really exist because there are no 99 sheep and there is no one sheep that was lost. In divine reality you don't quantify. There is only the harmonizing principle of God and infinite omni-action and good and that's all that really is there. What is in divine reality is not what we customarily think of in our daily lives. If we could come to see this, then we could transcend all of these fearful thoughts about these fantastic numbers and the question of no insurance or of how much insurance.

Dr. Hora: And how many sheep? Are they cheap or are they expensive?

Student: There are these numbers that you can get caught up in and frightened by. But since they don't really exist I did understand what you are saying to a large extent. It's still hard for me to understand how if we live in this world, which is governed by human laws and by human practices and human requirements for insurance, it is still difficult for me to see how it doesn't figure into the mix but I am going to try to understand it.

Dr. Hora: How will you do it?

Student: Well, it seems that in the past and even now when I contemplate the things that I am taught here, I don't know how, but they just seem to sink in and they become real to me, little by little. That's how we'll do it.

Dr. Hora: Who among you can remember that piece of stone, which an archeologist found in Egypt, and with the help of that stone he could read the hieroglyphs? The Rosetta stone. For thousands of years nobody could decipher the hieroglyphs on the tombstones or the pyramids and all the writings in Egypt. Nobody could understand what it meant and this researcher happened to find a solitary stone and on that stone were certain writings, which suddenly helped him to understand. With the help of the Rosetta stone, he could read everything that was written on the pyramids and the tombs in Egypt and ever since then, it is all open knowledge. Anybody who has studied it can read the complicated, fantastic carvings on these Egyptian monuments. It is an interesting side issue, because if you understand something crucial and of central importance, it opens up to you a whole world, which prior to that was a mystery. Nobody, for thousands of years, could understand what is written in those hieroglyphs. That man found this stone, the Rosetta stone, and that stone opened it up for everybody to read. Isn't that a fantastic story? Now there is such a Rosetta stone in Metapsychiatry. What is this Rosetta stone? It is not a stone. It is a discovery of the meaning of all koans. Zen masters were working for thousands of years with the help of koans. What does a koan tell us? It's a great secret, but if you understand the meaning and purpose of the koan, you can understand all the koans that were ever invented by the Zen masters for purposes of this teaching. If you understand this one koan, you can become enlightened every time you face up to a koan. So has this ever been explained to you?

Student: No.

Dr. Hora: It's very simple. Ask yourself. What is the purpose of a koan? What is the mystification that these Zen masters are always throwing at their students? They struggle for years and years in trying to figure them out and they never manage to figure them out. They get so disgusted and so frustrated that it makes the whole study of Zen very mysterious and arduous. It is simply this. The purpose of a koan is to help us to understand divine reality. There are thousands of koans that the Zen masters throw at new students and they all have one purpose. It's like the Rosetta stone. The purpose of the koan is to help us to get closer to God, and when we get closer to God, the more we understand divine reality. Without this Rosetta stone of Metapsychiatry, all the professors and religious teachers and leaders of the world are wracking their brains to understand what it is all about.

What was the mission of Christ? The mission of Jesus Christ was to help people understand God. The purpose of the Rosetta stone is to help people understand Egyptian history. Anytime somebody throws a koan at you, and life does it all the time, you can just start out by saying, "This is a message from God, coming to us from Jesus Christ in order that we might understand divine reality." So, if you keep that in mind as you approach a koan, you will become enlightened because what is enlightenment? Enlightenment, simply is understanding the nature of divine reality, the truth of being. You remember that we pray contemplatively, seeking to understand the truth of being. Now here is a koan, which says there were these 99 sheep and one sheep strayed away and the shepherd went and retrieved this sheep and there was great rejoicing. Whenever we understand a koan, there is a great sense of peace and gratitude because an incomprehensible mystery has revealed itself as the glory of God. Now what is the glory of God in connection with this particular sheep story? Once you understand the meaning of this parable, you will understand the nature of divine reality. So you are, to some extent, getting enlightened because you have understood the mystery of God. What is this mystery?

Student: Reality is perfect but seems imperfect because human beings have the tendency to think?

Dr. Hora: This story tells us we have to see reality in the context of divine mind, which is infinite Love-Intelligence. There are no partial divine minds. Everything is one, infinite, God, good, omnipotence, omnipresence, omniscience, love. So we are not going to particularize divine reality. Nothing can ever get lost in the kingdom of God because God does not lose his flock. Everything is one. You have heard me speak of the non-dual nature of divine reality. This particular koan says, "Don't worry about the insurance company." There are no insurance companies in God's kingdom. There is only perfection. There is infinity. There is harmony. There is the good of God. This is an important insight into the nature of divine reality. Once you understand divine reality, you are not going to speculate about one sheep or 500 sheep. There is no particularization. There are only sheep. We don't have to worry about the one that got lost. He did not get lost. You remember several times I told you stories where something got lost, I lost a little piece of metal and the way to find it is to stop looking for it and to acknowledge that in divine reality nothing ever gets lost. Everything is where it is and God can reveal to us where it is, provided we are not looking for it. What happens when we are looking for it?

Student: We can't find it.

Dr. Hora: Okay.

Student: We are thinking of it all the time and we are trying to figure out where it is.

Dr. Hora: We are losing sight of reality because in reality, everything is already there. It comes to us. It reveals itself and then we don't see just a piece of screw or something. We see that God knows everything that needs to be known all the time.

Student: This would apply to a sickness too.

Dr. Hora: A sickness, of course, yes, particularly the stock market. So just remember there is a Metapsychiatric Rosetta stone. The Rosetta stone of Metapsychiatry is that the Zen masters were trying to do the same work that Jesus was doing. He was constantly revealing the true nature of God and his creation. That is the work of the Zen masters, too. We are called upon to be here for God. So is anyone who pays attention to the meaning of everything. We want to become enlightened. That is enlightenment when you find a little piece of screw in the forest. The light has shined in your consciousness for a moment and there it is. We live in the expectancy of a perfect universe gradually revealing itself to us until we know and see everything as it really is.

Student: So in answer to the question of how do you come to know this?

Dr. Hora: You ask somebody, and he tells you that there are two intelligent questions. You don't start wracking your brains about how do you find 40 million dollars to pay to the insurance company for insurance. Then you could ask well how could God fix it for me, right? God is not worried about the insurance company. You need to understand that the purpose of these parables is that they lead us toward an understanding of God.

Student: If a problem seems unsolvable to us, the problem is a koan.

Dr. Hora: All problems are koans and they have a purpose. If you remember the Rosetta stone, you will understand the purpose of the koans, and the koans will reveal themselves to you in the form of "aha." Problems are lessons designed for our edification, and the more koans we can understand, the more enlightened we become, and certain miraculous events keep happening in our lives. So the Zen masters do not pray the way we pray. They do not recite words. They meditate, and meditation is focusing attention on the message, which the particular koan contains, and when this message reveals itself to us, we have made a step forward in the direction of the light. Otherwise the light shineth in darkness and darkness comprehended it not. The whole world suffers from a lack of comprehension. Even professors of theology at various universities have all kinds of rationalizations but they really don't understand.

Student: As soon as we look at something in particular, I mean whether it's a lost screw or a sheep or a problem, we have separated that out from reality.

Dr. Hora: Yes, we lost touch with reality.

Student: Last week we talked about interest and cultivating interest in Metapsychiatry. Could you make a parallel here between the growth of interest? Interest doesn't seem to be something that just comes all at once. As you say you take one step toward the light. Could you make a parallel with the fact that our interest grows slowly a little at a time?

Dr. Hora: Can you remember what was said here about the Rosetta stone? What was said? Now when you start out with a problem, this becomes a koan. Every problem is a koan. You remember that every problem is an interaction thought. That too is another form of the Rosetta stone. We have this

Rosetta stone. It is a little piece of stone, which you can hold in your hand.

Student: It's very big, the stone. It's huge.

Dr. Hora: I got the impression from the description. Well, the size doesn't matter. The purpose of it matters. Without this Rosetta stone, all Egyptian history would be in darkness. Nobody would know but those hieroglyphs are saved. Without Metapsychiatry, God remains largely unknown. There are all kinds of theological explanations of God, but they do not shed any light. If you are really interested in being enlightened, you start out by saying, "Dr. Hora said that every problem is a koan." It is a Jewish problem. (laughter) So, if nothing else works, try scratching your head. Maybe that will work.

Dr. Hora: Any questions?

Student: I know that it is important to try to meditate and pray so that some amount of understanding is allowed to come into consciousness. That is what I try to do and I find myself saying words, I guess, about things that I have learned here. That is the same as if I didn't see this program that you were watching; however, I have seen other programs where certain issues are being discussed where there is no communication or any kind of understanding and you come away from watching this blank. There is nothing helpful there, just a lot of words that sound very intelligent but have no context. So that seems to be what happens to me when I just listen. The only reason I know it is that I can see that when in the context of this parable and what you were saying here in group, something happens where peace descends on me. Sometimes there is a sense of assurance that is very different from when I am by myself. So the question is, where do you look or do you just have to keep asking questions all the time hoping that some day you will really understand?

Dr. Hora: Well you just heard what particular question one has to ask. What is the message in the koan?

Student: Let's say I am home and I ask that question. It's different when I am home than when I am here.

Dr. Hora: Well you are probably scared at home because everybody else is scared, but you don't have to be scared if you remember that the mystery is in your hand. You have the Rosetta stone and that will reveal to you everything you need to know. The doors of paradise will open up. It's a marvelous thing.

Student: There is a passage in the Bible that goes, "I shall open a door for you that no man will shut" (Rev. 3:8).

Dr. Hora: Right. Exactly.

Student: It's really beautiful.

Dr. Hora: You open it and no man will shut it. That's it. Again, you have to understand the purpose of the koan, of the mystery. You have to ask, "What is this trying to teach me?" Jesus was appointed by God to teach the whole world about divine reality. If you become a sincere seeker of the truth, you have the Rosetta stone in your hand and this will open to you the light and you will become an enlightened lady and no more will you have to speculate about religious teachings.

Student: When the meaning is not clear, is it appropriate to do nothing, be patient and keep mindful in trying to understand?

Dr. Hora: If the meaning is not clear, then the question is not being properly asked.

Student: Or sincerity or interest in wanting to know is not there.

Dr. Hora: Exactly. That's what I just said. That's what it means. Many times we are so insincere that we formulate the question in such a way as to avoid understanding, because we just love to lie.

Student: If we are scared, it's really hard to ask the question.

Dr. Hora: After being present tonight, you will never be scared because you know that the secret is in your hand.

Student: It's there. It's there.

Student: What if we are angry? What if we are mad?

Dr. Hora: Then we haven't understood this lecture because if this lecture is understood, you will be rejoicing over the lost lamb.

Student: So what is the meaning of the rejoicing? The rejoicing is . . .

Dr. Hora: It is gratitude. It is God who gave us this tremendous gift of seeing the light. We don't have to walk in darkness. "I am the light of the world; he that followeth me shall not walk in darkness but he will have the light of life" (John 8:12).

Student: Just to continue with the parable with the rejoicing of the lost sheep. The lost sheep might be this koan that has presented itself and that the rejoicing comes like, "Thanks, I needed that." You are just grateful. You have the ability to find gratitude for the fact that this lost sheep is exactly what is required.

Dr. Hora: When I was confronted with losing this screw assembly, I described it and I found it. It has no meaning to me, the screw assembly. But the fact that I was able to find it, that was the gift of God and that was a great joy. Not the value, the price of the thing. The fact that there you are in the forest, among all the leaves on the ground, and you say God knows where this screw assembly is and He will surely reveal it to me and I turn around and there it is.

Student: What is even more remarkable is creation's remarkable quality. But I mentioned to you a couple of weeks ago that I had not known that I had lost my keys when visiting you in Bedford Village. They had dropped out of my pocket and in leaving I just looked down and there were the keys amongst the pachysandra. If I had known they were lost I never would have found them. But even before I lost them I found them. (laughter)

Dr. Hora: The Rosetta stone itself must have been a tremendous joy for the Egyptologists, who had been wracking their brains over the many messages all over the monuments that nobody knew how to read. Here is this piece of stone and suddenly somebody could understand.

Student: We had the experience several months ago in London when visiting a British museum of being shown the Rosetta stone by a historian. She just described it again and again with excitement in her voice. She showed how the hieroglyphics were discovered through reading what was on this stone because it literally led them very logically to the discovery of what those hieroglyphics meant. She had such enthusiasm and such excitement in her voice in showing us this.

Dr. Hora: Yes, it is a great gift of God to this generation.

Student: You mentioned the issue of not being able to find the meaning and that there is not enough sincerity because we like to lie to ourselves. I can think of so many times that I have come for a meeting with you with what seemed like a problem to me and you have instantly seen that what I saw as a problem as I presented the circumstances wasn't a problem at all. I don't believe that I would ever have come to that awareness. Is that always lack of sincerity or is it simply lack of growth and understanding? Is the truth always available to all of us all of the time?

Dr. Hora: God does not discriminate. (laughter)

Student: Is it at every moment a question of sincerity?

Dr. Hora: Yes.

Student: I am trying to see the difference between the need to be sincerely interested in understanding and what actually leads to understanding. You are saying that God is not a punishment and reward system, meaning that if you don't understand you are not going to be punished. Or are you saying that if you do understand you won't be punished and if you don't understand you will suffer?

Dr. Hora: It is just a fact of reality that if you are sincere, you will find what you need.

Student: We can't be insincerely sincere; in other words we can't manufacture sincerity. We can't...

Dr. Hora: Oh yes, some people can be sincerely insincere. (laughter)

Student: And get away with it, you mean?

Dr. Hora: No. You don't get away with it. The motivations can be widely varied. There are people who go for years to psychotherapy and get nothing out of it because what they want to get is not valid. Most of the time they want power over other people. This isn't going to work — to acquire something that somebody else has or to impress somebody or to confirm oneself or to brag. There are millions of invalid motivations, which people seek in life and when you are obsessed with something invalid, you will never find the truth. That is why sincerity is so very important; otherwise, you are just wasting your efforts.

Student: Where I think I have encountered my insincerity is that when a problem presents itself, I had a thought of what is the solution to this problem. I was looking for the outcome, what I considered to be a healing of the problem. I am so set on that outcome that I am trying to find meaning there or whatever will logically lead there. The thing that I think has been most remarkable in my studies in Metapsychiatry is that outcomes really don't matter.

Dr. Hora: Right. Sincere seeking of the light is the right motivation. We are truth seekers. You know the first principle. Thou shalt have no other interest before the good of God, which is spiritual blessedness. If you are interested in something else that is not existentially valid, it cannot help. It hinders. Somebody said, "Why should I bother looking for the light when I am interested in money." But then all your attention is focused on making money. How will you find the light if you are looking in the wrong places? Let's face it, most people are preoccupied with invalid goals, those that are existentially not valid. The world will say, "If you are smart you will invest in real estate and they don't make it any more so you better buy." Then you put your mind to that and you are just misdirected. Seek and ye shall find. Knock and it shall be opened unto you. Ask and you shall receive (Matt. 7:7). All these Biblical sayings admonish us to make sure that we are focusing our attention in an existentially valid direction.

It reminds me of a broker who once tried to study Metapsychiatry and right at the first session he said, "I want to tell you what I want. I want sex and I want money." I told him you can't find it here. (laughter) That was the end of his study.

8

Spontaneity

Student: Sometimes we react to situations, or sometimes we respond to situations. Sometimes we calculate and think about situations beforehand. We have spoken about spontaneity before. It seems that if we're spontaneous we're not calculating. But then when we react, we're not calculating either. We reflect later and realize that we said something that was invalid. So what's a good way to be beneficial and aware of being a valid presence and, therefore neither calculating nor reacting, but being reflective and spontaneous?

Dr. Hora: It would be very helpful to admit that we don't know what this word means. Most everybody assumes they know what it means to be spontaneous. Hardly anybody knows, even after twenty years, after explaining over and over again, people don't know. It's a mystery, or, as it says in "The King and I," "it is a puzzlement." What is this word spontaneous? It's not calculative, it's not unreflective, it's not reactive; none of these things are spontaneous. If you step on a nail and you say "ouch," is the "ouch" spontaneous?

Student: It's probably a reaction.

Dr. Hora: Of course, it has nothing to do with spontaneity. It's a very interesting word. When you have an experience and you try to figure out how to deal with it, that's not spontaneity. That's calculative reasoning, isn't it? If you have an experience and you react to it, that's not spontaneity. That's reaction. So you cannot think and you cannot not think in order to be spontaneous. There is no human quality or faculty that can explain it. It's a total mystery. Smart people are not spontaneous. Stupid people are also not spontaneous.

Student: It seems that when we respond, that it comes through the grace of God; that no human or personal thing is happening.

Dr. Hora: Right. Now what is this grace of God that you are talking about?

Student: I can't explain it; it's just something that is. I used to think there were miracles; now I realize they're not miracles.

Dr. Hora: There are miracles everyday, all the time; nobody notices it.

Student: What is a miracle?

Dr. Hora: After we have explained this so many times! (laughter) Now what do you think of the response that out of left field comes a question and the response is appropriately present. What happened?

Student: Spontaneity.

Dr. Hora: So what happened? How is it that there is suddenly spontaneity in this room? How did it come in? Through the door? A human person cannot have spontaneity. There is just one quality of consciousness that can respond spontaneously, and it is a great mystery. It is the miracle of life and it is called love. Have you ever heard of this word, love? Love can respond with spontaneity. How is that? We know that fearful people cannot be spontaneous; angry people cannot be spontaneous; jealous people cannot be spontaneous; envious people cannot be spontaneous; rivalrous people cannot be spontaneous; ambitious people cannot be spontaneous. None of these behavioral human factors can manifest spontaneity. Love alone can reveal what spontaneity is. Do we all follow this?

Student: What is the definition of spontaneity?

Dr. Hora: It comes from the Latin, *sponte tua,* out of the will of God. When love is in our consciousness, God is there in the form of love and intelligence and that manifests itself as spontaneous responsiveness. It's non-personal and non-conditional and it is always benevolent. It's like a breath of fresh air, clarifying all the smog that normal human interaction generates. Next week I will ask you again, "What is spontaneity?" I bet you won't be able to answer. It's a difficult question to answer.

Student: So many times after various situations in life, you look back and say what might have been, what would have been more valid. "I shouldn't have said that." That's not even valid, but you wish it had been more valid.

Dr. Hora: A human person cannot respond spontaneously. Only love can do it. Now how is it that love can manifest itself as spontaneity?

Student: Because it is selfless. It is not a personal self.

Dr. Hora: Yes, because it is intelligent and it is spiritual and divine. If anybody doubted the existence of God, if this individual understood spontaneity, he would automatically acknowledge the reality of God. And certainly people who are agnostics or anti-God or not fully accepting the fact of God's existence have no way of being spontaneous. No way. It's always the human mind messing things up.

Throughout the history of art, there were great works produced. Who produced them? If we just judge by appearances, we see that Michelangelo was a man, maybe even homosexual. Yet he created all kinds of great works of art, of music and painting and sculpture, and we marvel how a human person could have this in him to produce such marvelous works. If we think that it comes out of a human person then we don't understand anything. A truly creative individual will tell you, "I don't remember having done this. It just happened." Something within the consciousness of the creative individual expresses itself in a certain way of beauty, honesty, goodness, and love; this is spontaneity. Great art always came about spontaneously. The great artists developed the ability of letting God work through them. They were very leery of accepting credit. Money, yes (laughter) but credit, no. All credit goes to God, infinite love-intelligence. It is the creative principle of the universe and is responsible for everything that is beautiful, good, intelligent and worthwhile in life. So whoever understands spontaneity understands God in action. There is a patient in Connecticut who has been suffering from being hard of hearing. He has gone to all kinds of doctors with his ears; he took his ears with him, and the doctors examined the ears and found nothing. And then we asked the right question: "What is the meaning of your difficulty in hearing what people are saying?" It turned out that he is a calculative speculator who isn't interested in hearing what people say, so he cannot hear. As the Bible says, "He that hath an ear let him hear" (Rev. 2:7).

Student: Dr. Hora, suppose you adhere to a certain value system, let's say, of honesty. Then, when there is a temptation to be dishonest, and you immediately reject that because you cherish the value of honesty in your consciousness, is that spontaneity?

Dr. Hora: No. That's commitment to the truth of being or the quality of character. It is mostly educationally derived, the result of the right kind of education.

Student: So it's a human trait?

Dr. Hora: No, it is a divine quality. The truth, as expressed through human behavior, is not an area of spontaneity. Spontaneity is closely associated with creativity and responsiveness to inspiration from God. You don't have to be a creative individual to be truthful or honest under all circumstances. Of course, if you are clear about spontaneity, you could never be dishonest or a liar. It would be impossible. That's part and parcel of the whole perception of reality. If we are dishonest or lying and deceiving ourselves, and others, then we are adulterating reality. So Jesus said, don't be an adulterer. Don't adulterate the truth of God. Cherish the truth and realize that all good comes from being here for God. We are here for God. We're spontaneous. We have inspired wisdom and we are non-conditionally benevolent. If we're not benevolent, everything is off. It's good to be good, right?

Student: In life, there are thousands of different situations that we encounter, so we'd like to respond appropriately. And they are all different and we can't know what's going to come and we can't know how to respond. If we meditate and understand what it is to have a loving consciousness, then that's what's going to make those situations just fine. We would be responding in a healthy way, in a beneficial way, and that love is what we practice.

Dr. Hora: Well, there are people who take courses in conversation and how to socialize, how to bullshit, how to sell, how to buy, how to deal with people. As Dale Carnegie wrote, "How to Win Friends and Influence People." These are artificial means of trying to approximate spontaneity and truthfulness. But it's artificial; it's nothing.

Student: Those things seem to be inauthentic. But if we accept the principle that "Nothing comes into experience uninvited," then the things that we encounter that the other student was speaking of, all those myriad experiences are being invited by our consciousness. So we really need to pay attention.

Dr. Hora: Yes. Our educational system is geared to what is called by a strange technical name: relationships. If you watch television or listen to the radio you will find this word "relationship" innumerable times. They are always talking and thinking in terms of relationships, which means interaction between individuals and others. And you go to school and learn psychology, sociology, good manners, street smarts and this smart and that smart and this is really an endeavor to sort of deal with the world on the basis of personal mind. And the harder you try, the more you study the more trouble you get into. All the marriages and the group experiences that people have invariably disintegrate because it is not possible to sustain harmonious communication on the basis of psychology. It is well known that, out of the entire population, psychiatrists and psychologists have the worst kind of marriages of all. And the more an individual is trained in psychology the more impossible it is for him to live and communicate harmoniously; because when he or she is positive it leaves an unpleasant aftertaste and when he or she is negative it results in conflict. There is no way that you can function in life on the basis of calculative thinking. That's what these things are and what they breed are politics and politicians. Calculative thinking drains their minds and they learn all kinds of things — selling themselves and selling things; it is full of suffering. It cannot be done. But if we understand spontaneity as a manifestation of divine love in human encounters, then we don't have to learn how to communicate. It is spontaneously there. And it's good and harmonious. It's free; it's effortless, reverent, and loving, based on awareness of the truth in all situations. We don't have to learn how to handle people. You see on television all kinds of schemes that people have devised to influence people, to sell, to convince, to seduce, to lure away, to pressure; all this goes on due to ignorance. People try to manage how they get along in this world.

Now if a hostess gives a party or has visitors, after the party there comes the reckoning. What I should have said, and didn't say! How should I have made this? Did I do it right? What did I say? What are you thinking now about what I was thinking? Was I right? Did I make a mistake? And then there are headaches and the inability to find peace. But true spontaneity is timeless, mindful, effortless, loving, and non-conditional. It's all forgiving, because God is infinite love and mercy. As human beings we can slip out of the spontaneity of timelessness, and mistakes may occur. But there don't have to be worries about it because it never really was. You made a mistake? No, it never was. The only thing that really is, is the presence of God, as infinite love-intelligence, and that's genuine spontaneity. You cannot take a course in spontaneity.

Student: Isn't this a course?

Dr. Hora: No, this is an iconoclastic course of everything else that isn't God. We are here to destroy the world totally, so that the presence of God may become clear. In this world you shall have tribulations, no matter what you do, no matter what courses you take, no matter how many psychology books you have read. It cannot be done. You just have to surrender to perfect love. In perfect love there are no persons. So it's no use trying to use your mind, or what you have learned or read in a book. In perfect love there is non-conditional benevolence. This includes compassion, forgiveness, peace, assurance, gratitude, freedom, etc. It's a whole 'nother smoke. People suffer so much anxiety when it comes to meeting somebody, friend or foe. Will I behave and handle this situation in the right way? Yes, spontaneity is a tremendous miracle of God in the human domain. So if we would like to function in the world we have to meditate on the question of what is spontaneity? If you meditate on this issue you may come to the point where it is tangibly present in your awareness and you function spontaneously in any situation, and that's good. And you understand that you don't worry whether you are liked, or appreciated, made an enemy, or criticized, or maligned in any way; it doesn't touch you. There is no reality to it whatsoever. Now what was your question?

Student: What is a miracle?

Dr. Hora: Spontaneity is a miracle. (laughter) A miracle is an observable event, which defies all customary ways of reacting or dealing with it; it's totally surprising and always good. All the healings of Jesus were miraculous. Now if someone understands something here or anywhere else, that's a miracle, because nobody can do it. Every time we understand a little bit, that's a miracle. If you understand a lot you are very happy, and blessed. The more we understand the truth of being, the more miracles will appear in our lives.

Student: It is difficult to know, if you are maligned, that it's not real. How does it come to the awareness that it is not real?

Dr. Hora: Well, does anybody know the answer to the problem of malicious thoughts?

Student: If you hear someone talking maliciously about someone else, or someone has been talking about your ideas, those kinds of thoughts seem hard to know that they are not real. You said that we can get to a point where we understand that they are not real and cannot touch us, but how do we know that and how do we come to understand that, beyond just believing the words?

Dr. Hora: Well it requires first a belief and then a conviction and then an understanding that God is infinite good and it is good to be good, and if someone is not good, but is malicious, then he or she is hurting himself or herself. And we don't have to do anything. We just have to be conscious of the fact that here is a phenomenon that falsifies reality.

Student: Einstein's remark is also relevant.

Dr. Hora: Yes?

Student: He said, "Arrows of hate have been shot at me many times, but they never touched me because they came from a world with which I have nothing in common."

Dr. Hora: Yes. What did he mean by that? They came from a world with which he had nothing in common.

Student: Well it is a world of interaction, and a world of personal-ism.

Dr. Hora: If you have learned this and have understood and you come across someone who is malicious, gossipy, and full of ill will, you have compassion for the guy because he is just hurting himself. He cannot touch you if your consciousness is not of this world but of omni-action. As long as we cherish relationships and interactions, either in families or business, we will be vulnerable to these things. That's why Jesus said that in this world we'll have tribulations. We have to transcend the world by knowing that these things are mistakes. People make mistakes and suffer from them and we don't have to suffer from them if we understand reality. We constantly pray and work and meditate and study to know reality. And here, this student asked this beautiful question about spontaneity and she tried to answer it and ran into an impenetrable, invisible wall of the truth. We all have to face the fact that nobody knew the answer. Was there anyone of you who understood spontaneity? If you were to ask a thousand people in church and out of church, in synagogue and in mosque, nobody would understand what it is. It is a miracle, a mystery. Spontaneity is a word, a beautiful word. Everyone believes that they know what it means. It would be a great blessing to know. But if we deceive ourselves, if we like to say, "I am right," we will just suffer. It is very important to know that if we understand spontaneity we understand God. What could be more important than that?

Student: It is interesting that the word "spontaneity" originates with God, and yet that component of its meaning or its origin is lost. If we look in the dictionary, this meaning would appear as a minor usage.

Dr. Hora: The interesting thing about this word is that no matter how many times we have spoken about it here, when it comes up again, nobody remembers, nobody knows, nobody has really attained understanding of it. It is easy to lose it. But if you don't use it you lose it. How do we use spontaneity in our daily lives? How do we use it, now that it has been explained to us?

(To a student) In your next party, visitors will come and may have all kinds of unloving fantasies. How will you use it? The way to use it is to cling to it tooth and nail. You have to cling to the understanding of what it is and pray that it works in you. "But the father that dwelleth in me, he doeth the works" (John 14:10). When our interest in perfect love is greater than personal success and power and influence and defensiveness, then it is there and we don't have to worry about it; it will be there. We are oriented toward letting it work in us. We cannot do it. But if we are imbued with the understanding of what it is, it works. It does its own work because God is God. "It is the Father in you who doeth the works."

Student: That's really helpful because that's the problem. We get distracted all the time. But if we just stay with that . . .

Dr. Hora: Sure, sure. Of course it is easier if we don't have to go to parties (chuckle), but some of us are forever going to parties and trying to like it, trying to make it a pleasant experience. But I think it is seldom so; parties always leave an unpleasant aftertaste because of the interactions which take place. You cannot make it otherwise.

Student: How is spontaneity different from PAGL? It seems as if aspects of it are in line with PAGL and compassion and forgiveness.

Dr. Hora: PAGL is the fruit of spontaneity. Or, as the medical establishment says, it's the side effect. (laughter) Isn't it interesting that everything that doctors do has side effects. "The good that I would I do not; but the evil that I would not, that I do" (Rom. 7:19). That's the godless experience of godlessness.

Student: I think I've lost spontaneity. I have to admit that I've forgotten what you said.

Dr. Hora: What? Already? You didn't wait until you got to the subway.

Student: Well, part of it is clear, that it is perfect love.

Dr. Hora: Right. And you know perfect love, so you have to practice, practice.

Student: So it's not different from perfect love?

Dr. Hora: It's a precondition to it; perfect love makes it possible. It brings into manifestation this highly desirable state of consciousness, called spontaneity. Practicing perfect love is really the easiest and the most wonderful discipline that we can apply for ourselves, except that you have to approach every day and every moment contemplating the importance of perfect love. It helps if you remind yourself that it is good to be good. You will become more and more spontaneous.

Student: It's good that you speak of a good that is good, that only comes through the grace of God. Because we are taught to be good and that is not good. And that's something we can do, but we cannot do the good that you speak of.

Dr. Hora: Well nobody said here that we have to do the good.

Student: No, what I meant was that the good that is beneficial just seems to come spontaneously.

Dr. Hora: So if we say, "It's good to be good," we are not talking about how to do it. We are making a statement about a mental orientation in life.

Student: I understand. This seems to also be something that just is another miracle; it's something that's a response. It comes from God only.

Dr. Hora: Anybody can be interested in being good. It doesn't mean that he has to produce this goodness.

Student: It's spiritual.

Dr. Hora: We have to be interested in goodness and if we're sincerely interested, it appears.

Student: A miracle.

Dr. Hora: Yes. Now St. Paul tried to do it and the result was this famous statement, "The good which I would I do not [he approached it operationally], but the evil which I would not that I do [again operational]." We're not talking about operationalism; it's a dirty word here. Yes, it's almost as dirty as relationships. In watching television, you listen carefully, and you can take a pad and make statistical studies of how many times within a span of half an hour or so you will hear the word "relationship."

Student: And also interaction.

Dr. Hora: Not so much, because it's fancier. But "relationship" almost anybody can use. It has become an epidemic ever since psychology became popularized and everybody forever talks about relationships. And the idea is that if you can handle relationships you'll be all right; so people are trying, but it doesn't seem to work.